The Warrior's Mind:
For Race Drivers

Be the commander on the battlefield of your mind

ENZO MUCCI

Thank you for all involved

If you love what is in this book then I would like to take the credit for that, but I cannot, because it all comes down to the mental training strategies that I learned from the seriously gifted race drivers, great coaches, successful individuals and from a whole host of personal development sciences that are out there. I would like to thank them all for their studies and dedication to human performance. It benefits us all.

I would also like to thank you, the driver, who has picked up this book due to your shared desire to be the best you can be. I truly hope that you can take something from the Warrior's Mind whilst on your racing journey.

And of course, I would like to thank all the drivers who I have worked with and learned from up to now, you have all contributed to this book in some way. One more, thanks to Chris Beck for doing the book cover design again.

CONTENTS

PART 4: ON THE BATTLEFIELD

A Heads-Up

Hello driver and welcome to The Warrior's Mind.

I am so happy to finally get this book out for you because I have been writing it, adding to it and redesigning it for over eight years prior to its release. The reason it has taken so long is because I wanted to make sure that I created something seriously effective and something that will make a difference for drivers who want to perform better.

Since the late 1990's, I have been an information hungry monster on the hunt for any knowledge whatsoever related to personal and mental performance and what you have here is a result of my findings.

As I was racing and doing what I could to learn from drivers like Nigel Mansell, Michael Schumacher and Ayrton Senna, I realised that most drivers could drive at a similar level and achieve similar lap times as each other, but the real differences between them was more to do with their mental game. It was plain to see that drivers like this would mentally operate at a different level compared to most.

I would speak to people who knew these drivers and others like them, and I'd ask things like "What separates them and why do they stand out?" and these people would all tell me something similar. They would always end up praising these driver's mental abilities and mindset, and the way they approached their racing, and it was down to them as individuals. These kinds of drivers had the mindset and attitude that would help them win so often and because of this they would be good at whatever they were to put their mind to.

This all stuck with me and it is why I have been so obsessed by the power of the mind.

Since those early days I wanted to learn as many mental sciences and therapies as I could get my hands on just so I could improve my own performance. As you have probably found, there are not many motorsport specific mental training programs around so I had to adapt them but I was over the moon when I found out that they actually worked. This was life changing for me.

Over time when you are studying all of this at the same time as competing and testing all the different types of mental disciplines you start to develop your own method, your own science and you come up with systems that work for you.

If you are the same as me and you have also been studying mental performance, then as you go through this book you will recognise certain exercises and strategies that are used in various personal development sciences.

You may have noticed that most personal development sciences and therapies share a lot of the same principles and fundamental teachings. Whether it be university standard sports psychology, NLP, CBT, the Silva Method, EFT or even straight up life coaching, they may go about things differently but when you look at their core structure, they are fairly similar.

You will also notice this about the many self-development books that are out there, they come up with catchy titles and the author will call it their own method, but they have just recycled teachings from the world of psychology that have been around for a long time. The answers are already out there for us.

So I collected and sourced some of the most effective parts of what they teach and re-moulded these strategies so they would work in racing.

The WM Mission Statement/Goal:

To give race drivers the ultimate secret weapon so they can perform at a higher level, overcome any challenge that dares to stand in their way and have a rare advantage in their sport.

This mission statement for the Warrior's Mind was at the forefront of my mind each time I would come to the computer to write. This would ensure that everything that I included here must contribute to that mission statement and give you the tools you need.

All the mental performance strategies that are shared within this book have been tested, re-tested and refined in the racing world with drivers I have worked with, so rest assured that the training techniques used here have been used at every level of motorsport, from karting to Formula 1.

What you will learn (or re-learn) here has worked, is working right now and will continue to work for as long as race drivers are around. That's before autonomous car racing takes over of course.

First things first

To start with I want to get a few things out upfront because when you read something like this book you need to have confidence in its effectiveness, and you need to know what to expect.

With that in mind I want to quickly tell you who I am and what to expect.

To kick things off formally my name is Enzo Mucci (believe it or not I am British) and I am a Performance Coach, which simply means that I mentally train people who want to improve their mindset and results.

Motorsport has been a big part of my life for some time now. I entered it just like you did, as a driver, but along the way I discovered my true passion for human performance and for helping people utilise the power of their minds.

This fascination started back in 1998 when I attended a personal development science called the Silver Method. This is a program teaches people how to access and use the Alpha state of your mind more, which is obviously beneficial for everyone to do.

After the first day of the course, I was completely hooked and wanted to learn more about the potential of our minds. Since then I have constantly been on the lookout for the next mental science to learn and try out.

Over my time in motorsport I have worn various hats (from being chief coach for BMW to being a sporting manager and coach of an F1 junior team) and in that time I have had the privilege of seeing things from many different angles and working with drivers as they face the spectrum of challenges that this sport throws at them.

Like many people who have been in this sport for a long period, you get to see and work alongside hundreds of drivers. In doing so you witness what makes some drivers succeed whilst others fail.

Just as with mental sciences, it is easy to start to see patterns and it is plain to see that the biggest area of opportunity for drivers, and what separates them, is their mental game.

This kind of observation allows you to create your own virtual playbook which makes it easy to help drivers and understand what they need to improve to create the career they want.

At the end of the day your mind is your operating system, and it controls everything you do so if you enhance and improve the way it works then you get better results.

Drivers can obviously improve their actual driving skills but again it is the mind that needs to digest, learn and execute those driving skills.

I found that it was not usually the ability of the driver that held them back, instead it was to do with their mental performance. They would either be mentally operating in a way that helped them progress or they would be set up with some form of internal performance blockers.

The beauty about us humans is that no matter what we are trying to achieve or improve, we individually remain the most important ingredient required for that to happen. For us to be at our best we must perform our learned skills with less friction and access our skills when it most matters.

Put simply, it is down to us individually to mentally perform how we need to, so we can produce the results that we desire.

My passion for sharing all this and helping people get what they want is what motivated me to put my teachings out there for all to digest. In creating the Warrior's Mind, I am hoping that the knowledge I have learned and picked up along the way will be helpful to you and whoever else takes the time to consume it.

What to expect here

If you are reading this then I know that we have three things in common, they are:

1. A shared interest for personal growth.
2. We expect more from ourselves than what we have shown up to now.
3. We are willing to do whatever it takes to reach our goal (ethically of course).

You are here looking for the advantage, to improve something about yourself and you have a goal in mind that you are determined to achieve. This means that you are a thoroughbred competitor, a true athlete and are hungry for success. How can I not respect and admire you for this?

I also appreciate and totally respect for where your mind is right now and for your willingness to do what most people will not.

As I previously mentioned, the origins of the strategies we will use here stemmed from a variety of therapies, personal development sciences, performance coaches, psychologists and people who have achieved outstanding results in their lives. I have modelled what works best and thoroughly tested it all with success.

Also, the Warrior's Mind will help you learn more mental weapons than most drivers have so another goal for this book is to help you become the Next Gen driver who can perform at an even higher level than what we normally see out there.

As you can tell, I dream big.

But again this is the outlook I have and the standard I am building this program with so it forces me to give you the best information and training possible.

The 'warrior' title is a metaphor, the real aim here is to arm you with the same psychology that a top warrior on the battlefield would have.

The Layout

The Warrior's Mind is split into four main parts.

Part 1 - The Warrior's Mind Philosophy - The heading says it all. In the first section I will talk you through the philosophy of the Warrior's Mind. This will help you digest what is being taught and give you the understanding needed to maximise and align yourself with the training given.

Part 2 - Your Awakening - Here we will see you in all your glory. Our objective is to unearth your inner warrior and get him or her to step forward and take the reins. We are going to get very honest in this part and face your demons.

The work we do in this section will carry on with us throughout the whole program.

Part 3 - Training Camp - This is where we will learn fundamental mental skills that will help you on a global scale. We will delve into the coding of your mind and set up your mental model, so it is specifically designed for the task in hand.

Most of the chapters in Part 3 are followed by a related training exercise so see the training camp, as a training camp.

Part 4 - On the Battlefield - Then we get to the specifics. These are the mental strategies that you can apply to help you whilst you are on the battlefield (on and off the track). We will cover a variety of areas from performance anxiety to improving your qualifying performance.

For this to work

The training in the Warrior's Mind is layered, it is designed to help you build up to mental mastery and to increase your mental skills as you travel through the program.

For this to work properly you need to complete Parts 1, 2 and 3 thoroughly.

Then if you wish to streamline it after Part 3, you can choose which areas in Part 4 are most urgent for you so you can use it like a menu.

Be warned, the teachings in Part 4 will not be highly effective if you have not fully digested the first three parts of the book. It just won't stick.

When it comes to the mind you need to master the fundamentals first to form a base, then you apply the specifics afterwards. That is the approach we will take here.

Ok that is it for the intro, if you are ready to get going then let's step into your Warrior's Mind.

The Warrior's Mind Explained

CHAPTER ONE

The Warrior's Mind Explained

> *Your mind is a battlefield, so be the commander*

First off it is not my intention to turn you into a blood thirsty savage and have you charging down the pit lane with a sword in your hand ready to maim your competition. That would not go down too well. Instead, the Warrior's Mind in our context is about giving you the mental attributes that have been modelled from the warrior style mindset.

To give you the full picture and explain exactly what is meant by the Warrior's Mind, let me explain what a race driver is and then I will explain what a warrior is.

What is a Race Driver?

A Race Driver is an individual who feels at home in an unpredictable and dangerous environment.

A Driver is a person who, whilst competing, is constantly making decisions that contribute to their success or failure.

Drivers are fully prepared to risk their lives and limbs whilst on the pursuit for victory.

When in a head-to-head battle, Race Drivers can remain resourceful and creative as they endeavor to outthink and outmaneuver their rivals.

A top Race Driver also has a high level of intelligence within their field and leads their team so they collectively advance.

What is a Warrior?

A Warrior is an individual who feels at home in an unpredictable and dangerous environment.

A Warrior is a person who, whilst competing, is constantly making decisions that contribute to their success or failure.

Warriors are fully prepared to risk their lives and limbs whilst on the pursuit for victory.

When in a head-to-head battle, Warriors can remain resourceful and creative as they endeavor to outthink and outmaneuver their rival.

A top Warrior also has a high level of intelligence within their field and leads their team so they collectively advance.

Not hard to spot the similarities, right?

Even though your specific goals, actions and physical skills massively differ from that of a thoroughbred warrior (or gladiator), you both require similar mental skills to succeed. Your opposition and challenges come in different forms, but to deal with these you need to have the same mental abilities as each other.

Emotional control and delivering under pressure are two main qualities that both of you must possess.

In learning from a warrior of war, or even from a fighter who takes to the Octagon, we are setting the bar high here so you can learn from the best and have much higher standards than the average driver out there.

I do not want to spend too much time learning from other drivers and teaching you what they do, instead we need to aim higher. Rest assured I have added the mental traits that are taken from previous true champions of motorsport and have incorporated them into this book, but we need to go further than that to ensure that we take things to a whole new level and evolve you.

Learning the mental traits and skills of someone like a warrior will help you do just that.

The specifics

To be slightly more precise, both you and the warrior share other personal attributes that enable you to get the results you want:

- You both problem-solve when you in constantly changing situation that has severe consequences attached to it.
- You both perform on demand when the pressure is on.
- You both outthink and outperform rivals who have similar skill sets and skill levels as you.

- You both have the self-belief and confidence to execute moves when needed.
- You both trust and act on your intuition.
- You both adjust and learn from recent mistakes without too much self-judgement.
- You both remain focused for long periods of time.
- You both strategize on the go.

Obviously, these are the kinds of things you do when you are at your best, but these are the skills to have if you want to be a successful warrior or a successful race driver.

For you to be able to do all this you need to use your mind in a particular way. These same mental attributes are also shared with competitors in other sports and disciplines such as Boxing, Rugby, Free Climbing, MMA and NFL.

One common thread that links all elite performers in sports like these is that they usually have a mindset that is also like a warrior on the battlefield.

This is not just for sports that are dangerous either, the very same can be said for true champions in most sports.

We all know the stories of sportsmen like Michael Jordan, Roger Federer and Cristiano Ronaldo. They may not compete within dangerous environments but these athletes and many more like them all had to mentally operate in this way.

It was their mindset that was the biggest differentiator between them and the people they compete against.

Who better?

Due to warriors of combat being the kind of individuals who need to have a high level of mental conditioning, who need to major in mental toughness and who need to master their emotions in order to survive, I chose the warrior as your guiding tutor due to the way they share so many similarities with you.

A warrior's mental performance bar is set very high because if they do not perform then they don't just lose a race, instead they can easily lose their life and the lives of their comrades. That is a huge responsibility which this forces them to perform when they need to.

If you want to be the best then we need to learn from the best, from the extreme version of yourself.

So who better to learn from and to model your mindset from, than a warrior?

Lessons From The Military

CHAPTER TWO

Lessons From The Military

> "You can never conquer the mountain.
> You can only conquer yourself"
> Jim Whittaker

Due to us creating the Warrior's Mind, who better to learn from than the military?

You can take a lot from how the military train soldiers because they take civilians and turn them into modern day warriors within a very short period of time. Also, during that short time they have taught these new soldiers the weapon and combat skills required to fight and survive in a warzone.

You could be an 18-year-old college student living the normal life in March of any given year, then by the time August comes round you can be a trained soldier fighting on the streets of a war-torn country.

To make the giant shift from being a civilian to becoming an active soldier in this time is quite impressive and requires a complete rewiring of the mind.

I am going to talk now as if you were joining the British army and I am giving you an insight for what you are about to face.

The army will put you through fourteen weeks of training and in that time you will be taught:

- Fieldcraft
- Skill at arms
- Military knowledge
- Battlefield casualty drills
- Combat based education
- The qualities of a soldier
- There is also rigorous fitness training thrown in there

Following this you enter a two-week course and when that is completed you are considered a trained soldier ready for combat.

The military are masters when it comes to changing the minds of people and to programming them for a certain task that is outside of the norm.

Meet the Drill Sergeant

When you enter basic army training your Drill Sergeant (or the Drill Instructor) is the person who is responsible for coaching, counselling and mentoring you through the program.

This may all sound fluffy and nice but in reality the Drill Sergeant has two goals, they are - **To break the civilian out of you and to give you a crash course in military lifestyle.**

For the Drill Sergeant to meet his two objectives he usually uses a heavy-handed approach which means that he will attempt to break your spirit as he metaphorically rests his military boot on the back of your neck whilst your face is in the dirt. He will shout in your face, purposely demoralise you and belittle you in front of the others.

This is all in the name of testing your will and helping you uncover your inner fighter. It allows him to see what you are made of and if you are in control of your emotions.

Once this is done and you understand that you can survive the mental and physical torment that they put you through, he will then design your training so it assists you in becoming the soldier you need to be.

The Drill Sergeant is there to completely wipe out your old mental programming and replace it with one that helps you become the best soldier you can be.

That means that he will take your current mental model, stamp on its face and assist you in installing a new mental model that will help you become a great soldier.

This is something that we will also do here within the Training Camp part of this book because for me it is vital for us to align your mind with what you want to accomplish in racing.

We must make sure that your mental programming isn't setting you up to fail and causing an internal/external conflict, instead we need to ensure that your mind is that of a warrior and is specifically designed to achieve the goals you have.

The Drill Sergeant must succeed

For the Drill Sergeant it is an 'absolute must' that he creates the mental shift within his cadettes otherwise he has failed, or even worse, he will create soldiers who are not capable of defending his country.

His whole reputation and job depends on his ability to turn them from people who live within the rules of a calm and safe society, into people who will put their life on the line for others, someone who will 'point and shoot' when the opportunity comes and someone who can think clearly when the pressure is on.

The mental skills needed to do these things are what you need as a driver. You are not going to shoot anyone, but you both share the need to possess the warrior's mind so you can succeed.

I think you know deep down that humans in general are originally coded this way. We care for others and have empathy yet we are also designed to do more than just work a 9 to 5 job. We are coded in a way that causes us to feel alive when in the face of danger, to come up with solutions to difficult situations, to complete tough tasks and we have an innate need for progress.

Society may drum into us that we need to create a safe life and avoid failure, but we are far more capable than simply following the usual school - college - job - pay taxes - and die life story.

If you are reading a book like this then I know that you yearn for more than the normal templated life story.

There is nothing wrong with living the safe life, many people are happy to live it and it is still tough to do, but for someone with your goals in racing, and in life, you cannot live by the general rules of society and expect great results.

Train as you will fight

A common saying in the military is "Train as you will fight".

This means that you will not sit in a classroom and just learn the theory of fighting, you will not just be tested on what a textbook tells you and then be given the qualifications that you want.

Instead, you will be in the field and given training that mimics and role plays battle. You will need to learn on the go and deal with public failure each day. You will quickly learn the mindset needed to remain resourceful when your body is exhausted, and you will take on the real skills that are vital when in combat.

I like this approach for racing as well because there is no point spending too long on theory, instead it is all about you learning the real skills that you need to become a fast driver.

Your training must be applicable, purposeful and closely related to the real world of racing.

If you use this kind of training then you build in confidence, you have more courage and you are much more disciplined. These are the traits of a successful soldier and of a successful driver.

Bodybuilding for the brain

The military sees the brain as a muscle, they get you to stretch it, to test it and widen your comfort zone so you expand it.

They discipline your mind by getting you up each morning on the strike of dawn (there is no snooze button), they are strict with your behaviour and your time keeping, plus they stick to rituals.

They help situational awareness and mental agility by organising random surprise attacks and by changing things up in the day. This keeps your mind alert and ready to adjust to whatever challenge comes your way.

They also teach visualization skills by giving soldiers a common goal and help them visualize what that goal looks like. They set triggers to remind you of that goal and to keep you focused on it. You embody the goal so much so that you are prepared to do whatever it takes to get it and it is always on your mind. You will even give your life for it.

As an organisation the military knows full well the importance of creating the mind needed to get the job done, they see it as the most important ingredient for success. That is exactly why their training is designed the way it is, it forces the army cadets to adopt the required mindset to thrive in combat.

This is not about survival; this is about building yourself into the person you need to be. In both your case and the case of a soldier, it is about becoming a warrior.

It's A Millimetre Sport

CHAPTER THREE

It's A Millimetre Sport

> **"**
>
> *"It's the little details that are vital. Little things make big things happen"*
>
> *Coach John Wooden*

Since I entered the coaching world, I have always looked up to and learned from previous great coaches like Cus D'amato from Boxing, Alex Ferguson from Football (or soccer depending on where you are from), John Wooden from Basketball and good old Bill Bowerman the Track and Field coach.

The way they taught, motivated and instilled discipline into their players to bring the most out of them fascinates me and will continue to be part of my life's study.

Another coach that I regard as one of the best is Hall of Famer Vince Lombardi. He was famous for his philosophy and for saying *"Football is a game of inches and inches make champions"*.

Football being a game of inches has multiple meanings, firstly the pitch they play on is measured in inches, feet and yards. Secondly his quote refers to the narrow margins that can sway the course of any given game, and thirdly it refers to the principle of how the players who take it upon themselves to fight for every extra inch, are the players who come out ahead. The inches add up, so the aim is to push for and focus on one inch at a time.

I have to be careful now because I am getting very close to doing a bad Al Pacino impression of when he was motivating his players in the film Any Given Sunday (if you haven't seen this film...watch it). He uses this all-time great movie speech to pump his team up whilst in the locker room.

Well for some time now I have had a similar view on racing and on life. But due to our sport being such a precision sport and us not really measuring in inches anymore, I prefer to see motorsport as a Millimetre Sport.

This refers to just how close things are and how slight changes to certain key areas can cause big differences in your results.

If you are racing round a circuit that has a lap time of one minute forty-five seconds (1:45), and you feel like you are miles off the pace because you are two seconds off that lap time, then believe it or not you are quite close to doing the same time.

You may be frustrated and feel as though you are way off the pace but if you look at things properly then you realise that you can bridge that gap with a few small adjustments to either you or the car (or both).

You will just be losing a tenth of a second here, two tenths of a second there, but nothing major. It is just an accumulation of small losses.

This is the same on the mental side, you can slightly change your focus in a race and produce a completely different performance compared to the way you were previously. Or with the car you may change the ride height by just one millimetre (1mm) and it can feel very different.

This also goes for your actual driving technique; you can slightly change your understanding for how that particular car needs a certain brake shape or throttle control and all of a sudden you find one second.

The first lesson I want you to take on in this program is that you are always closer to the answer than you think. Even when it looks like there is a giant chasm between you and P1, you will often find that the gap can be closed if you take the correct incremental steps.

Obviously, knowing what those steps are is the more confusing part but often confusion is the emotion that we experience just before making a new distinction or learning something new. The old brain does not understand but the new brain is just about to come up with the answer. We feel confused and even frustrated just before having an epiphany.

A lot of the time we just need to change things by a millimetre (that is metaphorically speaking here) and if you have gone in the correct direction then the results improve. Sounds obvious but this is a perspective that most drivers lose once they are at a race weekend.

When drivers are working on turning themselves or their season around, it is never an almighty shift in everything they do, it is usually just a couple of areas that need to be improved in order to see a leap forward in their results and performance. The skill is the ability to hit the correct areas and you must have the correct tools in place to improve these areas, but it rarely is an overhaul.

If we keep this outlook and stay on task then eventually you will get there and you will see a different outcome.

This millimetre philosophy can also be seen when you compare two drivers by looking at their data. I have had the privilege of working within the same teams as drivers Max Verstappen, Jules Bianchi, Daniel Ricciardo and Valtteri Bottas, and when they did a barnstorming lap or race, I would compare their data with their teammate and what you would find was often surprising.

It is surprising because usually when you open up the laptop to compare the data of someone like Max, Jules, Daniel or Valtteri to their teammate who may be off the pace, you don't actually see much difference between the driver's data traces. You would often end up saying something like "All we can see on the data is a bit here and a bit there".

It wasn't usually a night and day difference. I am not going to say that it was easy for the teammates to make these changes in their driving by the time the next session or race went green but it demonstrated just how close they were. If the teammate who is slightly off the pace kept motivated and remained calm, then they would take on the information that the data was showing and would start closing the gap.

Then they would hit the track and either be closer, as quick or even quicker.

The mind is often that missing millimetre

Usually, the area for these millimetres is found in the driver's mind. To improve their results they need to slightly improve something mentally and how they are personally operating.

You cannot really compare the driver's thoughts, perspective, emotions, focus, knowledge, concentration and intelligence on the data after each session, so that means that the mind is an area that is not really looked at.

When I say mental improvements, I mean that the driver may need to:

1. Learn or understand something new (about their driving, about the car or about the corners).
2. See and react to things differently.
3. Have the mindset that enables them to attack high speed corners.
4. Control their emotions more.
5. Improve their mental focus.
6. Improve their overall perspective and self-belief.

This list could be longer but in essence for a driver to improve they either need to learn something (and master it) or they need to mentally operate more effectively.

It will only be a slight shift from how they mentally operated in the past but these shifts can be complete game changers.

Always Remember

Even though it may externally look like you are way off, and big changes are needed, more often than not you are closer than you think to unlocking the results you want.

Mental Friction

When a driver is outstanding, it is obvious for all to see. They have a certain flare, you can see it in the body language of the car when they are behind the wheel and you will catch glimpses of the car dancing as they qualify or race wheel to wheel with other drivers.

I don't want to fall for the common trap of putting certain drivers on a pedestal here and say something like "True champions do everything better than everyone else" because that simply isn't true.

They do not score 10/10 in every area and some of the sports greatest drivers had some serious flaws to their 'game' and could have won many more races or championships if they didn't have these flaws.

However there is one main thing that most top drivers can do that most other drivers cannot, and that is to compete with less 'Mental Friction'.

When you work with an impressive driver, you notice that their mental coding and operating system helps them remove the kind of personal performance blockers that most other drivers suffer with. In doing so they can often express themselves through their driving. They have very few limiting beliefs or conflicting thoughts within them so they are a lot less busy in the mind thus allowing them to repeatedly perform at their best.

In essence they have less friction going on in the mind. They just go.

When a driver competes with less friction it's as if the car and themselves are one, they allow themselves to perform if you like.

If you have read the book 'In The Zone' by Clyde Brolin then you will remember reading many accounts of race drivers accessing their zone and driving in the flow state of the mind. This is a race driver's North Star when in a race.

To be mentally present, focused and to feel as though you and your machine are as one, is the holy grail. When you're driving well, when the car does what you want it to do and when you strip away any mental friction, then you let loose and perform at your absolute best. This is a bliss time for a racer.

It enables them to access their true level and have the so-called "spare capacity" to execute the qualities previously mentioned.

It is one thing to learn how to drive quickly, to learn the required driving technique or style needed or to fully know the circuit that you are racing on, but to be able to access and execute all this knowledge when it matters and in the heat of battle is a different story altogether. This is what the great drivers can do and when you marry that with high level driving ability, then you have a driver that stands out, an outstanding driver. Or at the very least you are about to see an outstanding performance.

You must design your mind for Motorsport

For you to have the advantage and to keep as many millimetres, centimetres and metres between you and the opposition, you must tune your mind to be tailored for racing.

This means to have the personal beliefs, perspective, outlook and mindset that is purpose built for what you want to achieve.

Obviously that is what the Warrior's Mind is going to help you do but you also need to live this every day. You need to continue to feed your mind with the knowledge and help it learn the skills it needs to become a real racing brain.

Your mind is in control of your whole body and its abilities, your mind basically runs the show, so you must make sure that the training you do contributes to the design of your motorsport mind.

Whether you are on the sim, in the gym, learning the engineering of your car, watching onboards, training emotional control or anything else, as long as you do each of these activities in a way that stretches your current capability and forces you to grow each time, then this is you mastering your craft and moulding your mind for the job in hand.

Most drivers never take the time to fully master their craft. They usually give it everything they have at race weekends but due to drivers only being at the track for between 10 to 20 weekends per year, they are part-time performers.

Kaizen

There are many 'Ways of a Warrior' that we will adopt in this book to help you improve your mental performance and one that we must adopt from the offset is based around the Japanese word Kaizen.

Translated to English, Kaizen simply means 'Improvement' or 'Change is better', but over time this single word has gained more weight to it than that. Kaizen has become a philosophy for any person or organisation that wishes to compete at the pinnacle of their sport or industry.

For them it means more than just improvement, it means constant improvement.

The Kaizen philosophy was implemented by Toyota following World War 2 and to this day they use Kaizen to make sure that they continually improve areas within the company, it forms a big part of Toyota's company ethos. Organisations have since copied this approach and have benefitted as a result.

If you are to make the gains that you need right now, then you need to train yourself with the Kaizen philosophy. A sportsperson such as yourself should do this but you will be surprised at just how lazy the typical race driver is.

In applying this to all areas of your racing life both on and off track you will keep making steps towards your goals, one millimetre at a time.

To be the best driver possible, you need to retain knowledge, you must become 'racing intelligent', you must be able to perform on demand and have the mental coding that allows you to drive how you need to.

The kind of training you need to do for this is full-time.

It may mean that you are only improving by 1% or by 1 millimetre per day, but these millimetres add up.

This sport will reward you when you hit the tipping point in your progression, when it becomes clear to see all of these millimetres add up from the outside.

In this program we are not interested in just chasing your dreams or results, instead the Warrior's Mind is going to help you become the person who automatically earns better results due to the way you operate.

Your Opportunity Is Now

CHAPTER FOUR

Your Opportunity Is Now

> *"Nothing is more expensive than a missed opportunity"*
>
> *H. Jackson Brown Jr*

I want to take a moment to help you see what's going on and how you can take advantage of what is happening right now.

As you walk around the paddocks and pitlanes you will witness what an 'ego culture' our sport is. After qualifying you will hear many drivers explaining the reasons for why they didn't achieve the results that they had hoped for. You can hear them saying things like:

- "My team isn't giving me a quick enough car"
- "My engine is causing me to lose too much time down the straights"
- "My chassis is too old"
- "I got blocked on my push lap"
- "My tyres just didn't come in"

You hear them reciting from the book of excuses as they try to prove that they are better than what their results suggest.

You may hear the odd driver nearly spit the truth and put the spotlight on themselves when they say something like "I made a mistake on my quick lap". This may sound like an admission, but this is often the driver still protecting their ego because they say it in a way to make us believe that it was a mistake that happened to them, so it's ok to dismiss.

They still fall on the side of being a victim and do not understand that they made that mistake due to their stress levels, their lack of focus, their mindset or other avoidable reasons.

They forget to mention that they made the mistake because they were panicking and braking later everywhere or tried to find all their lap time in Turn 1, which then caused the mistake.

Drivers often play this blame game for their entire racing careers and never truly look in the mirror or reverse engineer how they can change things and take control.

There are a lot of drivers who are mentally underperforming, they spend most of their careers paying for some kind of advantage and hiding from the truth. They do not take criticism very well and are not very good at performing under pressure. Anything that could potentially harm their image and the way others view them affects them massively.

Your Opportunity

This is amazing news because it gives a driver with the warrior's mindset the opportunity to really make a statement in this sport. If you approach your sport and train your mind in the way that is intended by this program then you will become the lucky wolf who finds its way into the chicken coup.

If you are in a sport where many competitors are hiding behind excuses and don't want to face their weaknesses (let's say it how it is, where most of the competitors are mentally weak), then as a person who is approaching that sport like a warrior approaches their craft of fighting, it's clear to predict that you will slaughter your competition.

If you do this correctly then as others are busy dancing around and disguising the truth, you will be welcoming the areas that you need to personally improve on and will be working tirelessly on those areas. This will mean that you will be advancing as most other drivers are effectively treading water and going nowhere.

Okay you obviously need to have the speed as a driver but if you have the warrior psychology in modern motorsport then you will always come out on top if you are competing against drivers with similar driving skills as yourself.

Tough Nuts

I don't want to tarnish everyone with the same brush because there are some seriously tough nuts out there still, but I am just seeing a lot more delicate minded drivers on the grids out there and want to bring this to your attention.

We have had drivers raise the mental toughness bar and who have shook the sport, drivers like Colin McRae, Ayrton Senna, Dale Earnhardt, Michael Schumacher and Max Verstappen are to name a few. When you come across drivers like these, you'd better be at the top of your mental game.

If you are not mentally prepared or equipped to face them then they will bury you.

This again is why I created the Warrior's Mind and why now is the time to improve this side of your racing game.

Manufacturers are looking for warriors

Factory teams are desperately looking for drivers who have the traits of those I just named.

They want to know that you can handle the pressure, that you are mentally stable, have what it takes to lead them to better results and will not harm the brand through your behaviour.

I want you to give yourself that chance and to become the kind of driver that manufacturers are looking for.

If you approach your sport as a warrior approaches their craft, if you continuously improve and understand how to mentally deliver, then you will massively increase your chances of success and you will portray the very characteristics that a manufacturer needs in their team.

Your character is of major importance when it comes to getting a paid drive.

If you have the discipline to stick to this then you will reap the rewards and you will experience just how much control you can have over your results and the destiny of your career.

If you want to go for this then let's head straight into Part 2 of the Warrior's Mind and awaken your warrior within.

PART 2
Your Awakening

CHAPTER FIVE

Your Awakening

"To make a fighter you gotta strip them down to bare wood"

Eddie Dupris

Now that we are in Part 2, it's time to get to work. From this point forward we are entering into your journey to become the person you need to become to get the job done.

Taking on a new mindset, changing your unwanted behaviours, leaving behind your old habits and enhancing your belief system is a big ask for any individual to take on and it is something that most people fail at.

So firstly, I want you to understand just how much commitment this is going to take. This isn't just you passively reading a self-help book, this is you taking on the challenge to evolve yourself within a short period of time.

If you do put everything you have into this then I know that you can change whatever you want about yourself. I can say that because we are talking about the No.1 influencer in your life here, we are talking about your mind.

Even though your brain only makes up 2% of your bodyweight it still uses 20% of the oxygen and blood in your body. That is a lot of energy required for such a small organ in the body.

It requires that energy to operate and power its 86 billion nerve cells (grey matter), it's billions of nerve fibres (white matter) which are all connected using trillions of connections (synapses). Information as electrical pulses are passed around the brain at speeds equivalent to 250mph. That's the kind of speed that even an IndyCar oval racer would be proud of.

This organ that you have behind your eyes is the closest thing we have to a miracle; it is the final frontier of the human body that our best scholars still cannot fully understand. The human brain is having a hard time working itself out.

What we do know is if we can operate it in a more efficient way using proven techniques then we can get ourselves to perform better.

That is what we are going to do here.

It is a big promise but if you commit to this and you start to train yourself using the proven techniques that we are going to use here then you will set yourself onto a journey of self-discovery that will help you be at your best, when you need to be.

Digging Deep

To begin your journey for the Warrior's Mind, we need to start by grabbing hold of your imaginary spade and trust it into the ground. We need to use Part 2 to not only unearth the real you, but whilst doing that we need to lay down the strong foundations that will enable you to truly build the mindset that you want.

For you to create a different mentality on the global scale, you must be prepared to delve into your core, to go deeper than just the surface. We can all change our mood temporarily, but for you to become the kind of person who can reach your goals and then you must start to re-code your thinking from a deeper level.

We need to dig deep into your mind to make sure that we plant the seeds that will help you grow deeper roots. These new roots will help secure the mental work we will do later and help your new mindset withstand the test of time.

Ignoring this will be as effective as a painter repainting over an old barn door expecting it to look like brand new again.

If the old barn door is weathered with its previous paint flaking off, and the painter simply paints over it hoping that it will be good enough, then it won't be long before that new top layer starts to flake off as well revealing the previous paint again. Back to square one.

However, if the decorator was to take the time to sand down that door, to treat the wood, to prime it and then repaint it, he would then be looking at a door that has transformed. That can now brave the weather, operate correctly and look good for some time.

This is the same for you.

As the covering quote from Eddie Dupris states (taken from the film Million Dollar Baby):

"To make a fighter you gotta strip them down to bare wood".

That quote is relevant to you right now. If you want to change things about yourself then we need to go deep. Don't worry, we are not going to delve too much into your past because again that has to be done in person, but we are going to do what we can to help you strip things back to bare wood so you can then build yourself back into the warrior you want to be.

Your Awakening

To start this 'stripping' process we are going to start by taking a true look at yourself in the Destiny Mirror, then we are going to fully understand your reality and show your mind exactly what needs to be done in order to advance.

Then we will beckon your inner warrior forward. To awaken the person you know that you are already deep down and to give them back the reins so they can direct things going forward again.

The Destiny Mirror

CHAPTER SIX

The Destiny Mirror

> ❝
>
> *"Our destiny is not written for us, but by us"*
> *Barack Obama*

As you can tell I like giving things titles and the Destiny Mirror is another one. It sounds kind of mystical, and it is.

This has to be one of my favourite and most powerful mental techniques that I've got within the mental toolbox because this one exercise can help you change your life and can be used for so many different purposes.

Whilst reading this book we will keep coming back to this mirror and to use what we see within it.

It can be the pivotal point where you decide which direction you're going to go, who you're going to become and it allows you to see how things could well play out in your life.

On top of this it gives you another way to take a look back at your past, at how you've been acting up to now and where you are right now. I told you this was good.

We can make this as painful and as pleasurable as we want but first I want you to understand that there are three main parts to the initial Destiny Mirror technique and I have split them over the next three chapters.

It looks like this:

Chapter 6 is obviously called Destiny Mirror and this is where we will plan your path forward and set up the attributes you need to acquire.

Chapter 7 is where we take a look at your true reflection, we look at you in the mirror and see how you've been performing up to now.

Chapter 8 is where we summon your warrior forward to make sure that we start to create the required mindset.

It's time to get clear

It is always a good thing to start mental training by getting clear on you and your past, present and future. This helps us paint the picture correctly and from there we can build the person you want to create.

After this section you will know fully what needs to be done. We will show your mind how this game is going to be played and then we'll get the specific tools that you need to actually go and do this.

The Destiny Mirror

The Destiny Mirror exercise requires you to use your imagination and a tiny bit of visualization. This is actually good practice for when we get into visualization later in the book.

To do this properly (like many exercises within this program) you will need to close your eyes as you use your imagination but due to this being a book, it's kind of hard to read and close your eyes at the same time. Impressive if you can.

So for this reason it is obviously OK to read it through first and then close your eyes to perform it, or do your best to imagine things in between each direction, or get someone to read it out to you whilst you close your eyes and go through it.

Caution: Each time you do a closed eye exercise within this book please make sure that you can do it safely, and you are not operating anything that needs your attention elsewhere of course. This is to help you, not injure you. You'd be surprised at the amount of people that will try this whilst driving on the road, please don't.

By the way, if you get yourself over to the Warrior's Mind website then you will find the Warrior's Mind Workbook that you fill out as you do these exercises. Go grab it if you can.

I am now going to walk you through the eight steps of the Destiny Mirror.

Step 1 - The Mirror and your Timeline

I want to introduce you to your Destiny Mirror. We can use this imaginary mirror for all different kinds of visualization drills from mental time travelling to self analysis.

When you are ready and when you know the instructions, close your eyes and imagine that there is a huge mirror in front of you. It has a big and impressive looking gold frame around it and is a similar mirror to the ones seen in the Snow White films, when the Queen is asking it "Mirror mirror on the wall, who's the fairest of them all?". Or similar to the mirror in Shrek that Lord Farquaad uses to get certain answers.

Your Destiny Mirror is similar to what they had in these movies but you are not asking for who's the fairest or trying to get some answers that way, not just yet anyway, what we're going to do is look into your Destiny Mirror and imagine that you can see a timeline within it.

Your timeline is a horizontal line that goes from left to right of the mirror and shows the journey of your life.

Your timeline begins on the far left where the actual starting point is the day you were born. Then bang in the middle of the line is where you are right now, the current time, and then everything that is right of centre, is your future.

Your past, which is obviously left of centre, is practically set in stone and we can't change what has happened but we can see moments from your past and using this timeline we can revisit earlier times from your life.

Then when we come to the future portion of your timeline, this is the area we can use to see how things turn out. This is the destiny section of your timeline.

We don't know how long this part of your line will go on for but we can play with it, adjust it and use it to design things.

So there it is, this is your life on a timeline in front of you. You can either do this exercise by putting pen to paper and drawing it out if you want to physically see it or you can use your imagination and visualize it. Whichever way you do this, we are using this timeline to help you become clear on things and see your life in a more detached way.

When you see your life from this angle and point of view, it helps you see things in a clearer way with less emotions involved. To see your life in a more detached way like this helps you make better decisions and can be used to reinvigorate your motivation.

Like the popular saying suggests "You can't see the wood for the trees", this is our way of preventing the common trap of being too close to our problems. It is good to take a step back so you can see the truth. This improves your self-awareness and helps you self-coach yourself.

If you want your timeline to be more zoomed in, so you have to literally put your head into the mirror to see it all, or if you prefer to hover over your timeline so you are flying over it, then this is totally up to you. See your timeline from whatever angle works for you, this is yours to design.

The main thing here is that we have a timeline that shows your life, you imagine it however you want.

Step 2 - Follow the line

As you look at your timeline now, you can follow your life from your birth and walk the line with your eyes and see memories as you grew up.

After your birth you will have a small empty area before having your first ever memory. Then as you make your way right you see that time when you were around five years old or so, then other memories as you chronologically travel across your lifeline.

You don't have to revisit many memories for now, but as you slowly scan from left to right, following your journey up to now, you can fill that line with memories just like an old slide projector has picture slides within it. Each slide is a memory.

Or you can pop in little flags along your past timeline that mark different memories.

For now though we are going to talk about your destiny, so our work will mainly be focused on the future part of your line. We will come back to your past later.

Step 3 - Claim your North Star

What is the big goal that you have in racing?

What is the one thing that would be your dream outcome for your racing and something that you wish will happen?

We are going to call your big goal your North Star. This is the whopping goal that you would love to achieve and is your long term racing dream. It is the type of personal goal that gets you up in the morning and what you think of most.

For some this may be to make it as an F1, IndyCar, NASCAR, WEC, WRC driver or a MotoGP rider. Or if you are already one of those then maybe your North Star is to become world champion.

A warrior is only as good as their purpose. The more they are shooting for in life, the more they have to become. So make sure that your North Star is the kind of goal that forces you to step up and is a big ask. The kind of goal that will require you to grow as an individual to even stand a chance at getting it. So choose a North Star that is a stretch, but is still possible if all went well.

I've always preferred to call our major goal a North Star because it acts as your guiding light, if you stay focused on it then you will make decisions based on it, you will take actions that take you closer to it and you will turn yourself into the kind of person who can attain it.

This is all perfect when you are determined to possess the warrior mindset. You need that North Star to be your guide in all areas, without a goal like this your inner warrior will wake up. There will be no need for them to.

Pick your North Star now.

Once you are happy with your North Star, I want you to visualize it. We need a victory scene of the actual moment when you achieve it. You may be signing that big contract and shaking the hand of the team boss, you may be on the top step of the podium or accepting the championship trophy at the awards event.

Imagine what it will be like when you achieve it, also get yourself to feel the emotions that you will feel when there.

Take the time to experience it, as if you had accomplished your dream goal. Put a smile on your face and go there mentally, feel it, breathe it in and again allow your mind to flood itself with the emotions that you will feel.

We need to attach emotions to your North Star because emotional energy will allow your whole mind and body to be connected to it. We often have big dreams but rarely do we take the time to feel and experience them, so we don't associate with them properly.

If you are serious about achieving such a goal then you need to embody it and it needs to be a part of you.

Take the time to do this now.

Step 4 - Capture and place it in

Once you have your victory scene for when you reach your North Star, I want you to capture that scene as a still image, or even a short movie of that time.

This snapshot would be like the kind of photo that someone would take of you just as you achieved your dream. See it as if it were on a polaroid picture or as a GIF if it is a moving image.

Once you have it, I want you to shrink that image down and put it onto your future timeline.

If you want it to happen in the next ten years, then just guesstimate where that would be on your destiny line, you don't have to get the measurements right here, you just need it in the future.

Some people choose to have it at the very end of the timeline, but I like to think that life will continue after the goal, but again, this is your timeline and you make the rules. Do what feels right for you.

As you look at your whole timeline you can see your own story so far and the place where you want your future story to go.

Step 5 - Claim your first quest

We are going to do a similar exercise now, but this time you will do this process for your more immediate goal. The goal that you want to have done by the end of the season or within the next twelve months. This to be the first major milestone for you whilst on your pursuit for your North Star.

We will call this goal, your first quest.

Warriors are usually on a mission, on a certain quest that they are determined to complete. They have been given orders to bring back that princess, to go find that treasure, or to win the battle.

This is the equivalent to you and your first quest.

So what is the first quest that you need to complete in order to take you closer to your North Star?

To give you some examples, this may be to win a race, win a championship, get the much-needed sponsorship together to compete next season, or any other fairly large goal that must be accomplished within twelve months.

Once you have it, like before, visualize it and create a victory scene of when you complete that quest. See what you will see, hear what you will hear and experience it now.

Put a smile on your face and feel it, live it for a moment.

Step 6 - Capture and place it in

Take a mental snapshot of your first quest's victory scene.

Capture the emotion and moment, then shrink it down and place it on your timeline closer to the centre line.

This may help you correct the proportions of where your North Star sits but this is all good, the more we start to populate your timeline the more precise you will become.

As you take a step back and look at your timeline this time, you have a more structured look to it and you can see a stepping stone in place that helps you get to your North Star. This is the start of us designing your destiny.

Learn from what they say

You will have heard many people comment on the importance of having a vision of your goals and what you want out of life, here are just a few.

Arnold Schwarzenegger said **"Create a vision of who you want to be, and then live into that picture as if it were already true"**

Conor McGregor said **"If you can see it, and have the courage to speak it, it will happen"**

Will Smith said **"Our thoughts, our feelings, our dreams, our ideas are physical in the universe. That if we dream something, if we picture something, it adds a physical thrust towards realisation that we can put in the universe"**

Muhammad Ali said **"Champions aren't made in the gyms. Champions are made from something they have deep inside - a desire, a dream, a vision"**

When the people who have already achieved their original dreams keep preaching the same kind of messages, then you have to take note.

Seeing things clearly helps us on many levels, it dictates how we train, what skills we learn, how we apply ourselves, the actions we take, the decisions we make and the person we become.

That is precisely why we are starting with this exercise because it will allow us to initiate the emergence of your Warrior Mind.

Step 7 - Mark your current location

For the last part of this exercise I want to bring your attention to the centre of your timeline, where you currently are in life right now as you read this.

If you want to find out directions for a place you want to end up, then you need to know your current location in order to do that.

That means you need to get clear on where you are right now and the situation that you are in. When I am working with a driver one on one this is where we do a full assessment, but because you are coaching yourself here we will just keep it down to the basics of answering where you are now.

What is your current level as a driver?

What are you racing?

How much budget do you have for racing?

What championships or results have you accomplished up to now?

Where do you stand in the motorsport world?

Whether you are a complete beginner or you are in F1, we must ensure that we have an accurate current location because this will form your starting point and it will help you see what needs to be improved in order to complete that first quest.

It will also set up what we will do in the next chapter.

Visualize your timeline again and put in your current position. Have a scene that pretty much sums up where you are now, take a snapshot and place it at the very centre of your timeline.

Step 8 - What's it going to take?

You can now see everything, you can see parts of your past, where you are currently and where you are determined to end up.

This creates a very clear path and your mind has already started to fill in the gaps going forward and it will start to plan the kind of things that you need to do and who you need to become so you can reach those future goals.

This is great, but we need to do this consciously now. We need to come up with the core skills, knowledge, mindset and attitude based qualities that you need that will help you go from where you are now to that North Star.

Name the attributes needed

I want you to think of at least three personal traits that you must possess if this is all going to happen.

What external skills do you need?

What kind of mental skills do you need?

How much do you have to apply yourself each day?

Come up with a small list of things you must be good at in order to make this possible.

To help you do this, think of someone who you admire, who has already achieved your North Star.

It may be Dale Earnhardt, Mario Andretti, Lewis Hamilton, Sebastien Loeb, Valentino Rossi, Travis Pastrana, Nigel Mansell, Michael Schumacher, or someone else. That person could be a successful race driver or someone outside of our sport.

Maybe think of someone who had an even lower starting point compared to your current position, yet still made it.

Once you have them in mind, what personal qualities made them different to most other people?

What made them different and helped them win so often?

What was it about their personality or work ethic that helped them?

Write these down on a piece of paper in the Warrior's Mind Workbook, or if you cannot do that, just remember these three attributes and keep them in mind for the next chapter.

Once done, move on to chapter seven and this is where we get to take a look at you.

Your True Reflection

Your True Reflection

> **"**
> *"Facts do not cease to exist because they are ignored"*
> *Aldous Huxley*

It's time to look into that mirror again but this time we will use it to look at yourself and see things for how they really are.

We will start off with those three or so qualities and attributes that you listed or thought of just now. Then with those attributes in mind, I want you to look back on your timeline over the past six months or so and score yourself out of ten in each of them areas.

As an example if you put things like:

1. Relentlessness
2. Supreme confidence
3. Outworking everyone around

Then you would score how you have been performing, out of 10, in these areas. How relentless have you been, how much of your confidence have you demonstrated and have you really been outworking everyone?

Score yourself in each of the areas that you came up with in the last chapter.

Again, be truthful here. If it helps then ask someone who knows you well to score you, someone from your team or family.

Let's just say that 'self-belief' was one of the traits that you regard as a seriously important ingredient to help you achieve your North Star.

If you look back and realise that you always lack self-belief, you find it hard to speak your mind, get embarrassed easily when someone questions your viewpoint or are not sure whether you can make it, then you would score yourself around 2/10.

If you have self-belief but only at certain times, then you would score yourself around 5/10.

If you are always busting at the seams with self-belief and always back yourself when in and out of the car then you would be nearer to 9/10.

Do your scoring now and then come back to the book and we will continue to look into the mirror to find out more about you.

Your recent performance

We will revisit your scores later in this chapter but for now I want to unearth some of the mental traits that you want to personally improve on, the things about yourself that you know are below par and are not good enough to help you attain that North Star.

You may have already mentioned them in the scoring section, but to make things even clearer I want you to go back over your past and pick specific times when you mentally underperformed.

Times when you know you should have gotten a better result or outcome but due to the way you were that day, due to the way you were mentally, it just didn't go to plan.

If you haven't raced for some time then pick a time away from the track, even if it was whilst you were racing online on your home sim. Or even if you pick moments from your everyday life away from racing all together, this is all applicable.

You can look back on your timeline if you want to refresh your memory and replay these moments by going into these memories and watching it happen again and feeling what you felt back then.

When you can fully recall a moment or two like this, I want you to answer these questions:

1. What emotions were you feeling at that time?
2. What were you thinking about when you were not performing as you wanted?
3. What were you worried about?
4. What were you focusing on?
5. Why did you underperform?

These questions will help you get to the route cause of why you didn't drive or perform as you should have.

This is great information because looking at these times tells you a lot about what you will need to improve and what will happen if you don't improve. This is self-awareness at its best right here.

You will have obviously had some good performances in these times but if we are to create the Warrior's Mind and be the best we can be, then first we need to understand our 'so called' flaws.

We will spend time on our strengths later, but not just yet, first I want to show your mind that things must change if you want to advance from here.

Play it out

By taking a look in the mirror at your reflection like this we are seeing things for how they really are and we will expose the areas that must be improved if you are going to reach your North Star.

Next, we will see how things will play out if you continue to score what you have scored and if you continue to have these moments when you are not mentally performing as you need to at critical times.

It is time to get tough on yourself and add some pain here because your big goals are going to take some serious effort, and most of that effort will be within your own mind.

Take a look at your Destiny Mirror now to see what happens.

Use your imagination again and answer this question - ***What will happen in one year's time, worst case scenario, if you continue to score as you have been in these vital areas and continue to have these times when you underperform?***

Are you likely to achieve your first quest?

What will it look like?

What will people be saying and what will it feel like in twelve months when you haven't achieved anywhere near what you wanted?

Yes, I want you again to make this as painful as you possibly can. This pain is to drive you, to shake your mind out of the way it has been performing up to now and be motivated to change.

Warrior's always need to see things for how they are and prepare for the worst. This is us doing just that, so take the time to make this as painful and as disgusting as you can.

To add more pain let's go two years into the future and see how bad things can get then if you continue to underperform and do not act as you need to. Will you even be racing then?

To keep piling on the brown stuff, jump to where you put your North Star (if it is more than two years away). If for example that was around six years from now then how bad do things look then?

What will your life be like then if you allow your mind to drag you down and suffocate your success?

This is more likely than you think

It's easy for us to think "Ah it's ok, things won't get that bad" but just think about this.

All you have done here is explained the kind of outcomes that many drivers before you have created, so it is perfectly possible that this can happen to you. Actually, the outcomes that people explain when they do this are often more likely to happen than them reaching their North Star.

You may well be already walking this 'worst case scenario' destiny line. If again you take your scores and play that out you can see that you may actually be going down that path.

Far more drivers fail due to their mental coding than you would like to think. They may blame their team, their lack of money or bad luck but most drivers who underachieve are only really being held back by their mentality.

Their mental skills didn't help them overcome the challenges that they faced so they quit. I have seen this happen a thousand times already.

Let this drive you

This whole exercise is to start the wake up phase, to help you wake up your inner warrior by rubbing your face in the things that could kill your racing career.

Motorsport is a brutal sport, if you are not mentally ready for it then it will expose you and people within it will bleed you dry. The Warrior's Mind isn't just a play on words or a catchy title, it is the very mindset you need to survive this blood fest.

You may think I am over dramatizing things here but just think about the number of drivers who make it as a professional driver nowadays...not many. That is because it is bloody tough and only a few drivers deserve to make it.

If you train in a way that faces your flaws and with a mindset that understands where it is at, what it needs to improve on and what it needs to become, then you have the basis of moving forward and becoming the person you need to be.

Do this part correctly and you will start to wake up your warrior.

Summon Your Warrior

CHAPTER EIGHT

Summon Your Warrior

> **"**
>
> *"Step up or step aside"*
> *Christopher Titus*

You now have a choice to make about your future. You have seen your two different destiny lines that could very well turn out to be your real lifelines.

Next you need to decide on the kind of person you must become if you are to stand a chance of getting to your North Star and can deal with travelling along that line.

Or you can decide to keep going as you have been up to now, or even quit racing all together if you think it is too much of a tough challenge.

You are always in control of your decisions. When you take a snapshot of your situation and see what is going on in your life and what can actually happen, it can make you revaluate things.

It forces you to ask yourself questions like, "Am I up to this?", "Can I change myself?" or "Is it really possible?".

These kinds of questions come in and the answers you give to these questions are vital because they will direct your actions.

If you decide to pack up racing because you conclude that it is too big of a task and you cannot see yourself turning your scores of 5's into anything near 10's, then great, we have just saved you a lot of time and money. There is no shame in this and you can focus on something else that is more important to you. Remember that this book is here to help you be the person you need to be, if racing isn't the perfect fit then you can still apply all the techniques shared in this book to better yourself at whatever you do in life.

If however, you are a crazy individual and still want to scale that mountain and want to learn all the personal performance skills to help you do that then it's time to fully commit to this and give it your absolute all.

If you think that you have been working hard up to now then I want you to see that as child's play. You are going to need emotional fuel to get you up this mountain and blind faith to guide you as you complete one quest at a time on your treacherous trek to your North Star.

You are going to take some serious hits on the way so we need to make sure that whoever you become going forward, that it is the kind of person who can deal with those hits and still remain focused and is able to execute no matter what.

This is going to take everything you have, and some. But if we give you all the personal skills that the people had who travelled your route before you, and you put the work in and improve your skills, then why the hell shouldn't you reap the same rewards?

As long as you keep building both your career and your mind each day, then eventually you will create something. We're going to talk about building your mind soon but your future is also built the same way.

Each day that you complete should be seen as another brick added, so make sure that these days are purposeful and maximised.

To live this way, you need to adopt a warrior's approach. It must be your inner warrior that wakes you up each morning, not the person who presses the snooze button.

It is amazing what people can achieve in a lifetime. It is also amazing what people do once they decide to really go for it and decide who they want to become to do that.

Once you get yourself to the tipping point where you fully commit to a goal like this, then you can feel the energy, determination and focus bubbling inside of you.

That feeling is your inner warrior. That is them waking up. It is your job to keep that warrior awake and keep them in control for as long as you can.

Your inner warrior must come out and take the lead. You have got no choice because if you are committing to this then your old self will not be able to do it, so you have to reinvent yourself. You must bring in the skills of the mind that allow you to maintain the warrior traits.

Now is the time to get that inner warrior to step up.

I want you to remind yourself of your Destiny Mirror each day. Use it to keep you on track, to analyse how you have been performing over the past week or so and use it to remind your warrior what they are assigned to.

Then at the end of each week you can ask "Have I been and done enough this week?" and if not then you find out what must be done the following week and what skills you need to improve to do that, mental or practical skills.

This is where the Destiny Mirror helps you walk the path you want and keeps an eye on things.

Be relentless and disciplined

This will take relentless conditioning and conscious upkeep from your side. Each day you must summon your warrior to step forward and set them to task. If you spend too many days, or too many weeks allowing them to lay dormant then you will be back to square one before you know it.

Discipline is one of the main traits of a champion (a warrior), so if you are to wear that identity then you must prove that you have the discipline and follow through.

Every time you meet a bit of a mental performance block, you deal with it.

If you experience lack of confidence from time to time then you say "Right, how am I going to build confidence today?".

Obviously the skills within this program will help you do that and we're going to cover emotions later, but whilst on the go life will throw you challenges that test you and you will need to deal with them.

If you need inspiration, then look again to those who have walked your path already and search for the answers you need. This is a lifelong pursuit and something you will always be conditioning. The warrior lifestyle never stops, you will apply this to whatever you do after racing.

Learn from yourself

During the tough times you can also use yourself as a model to learn from. When you are struggling with something you can reawaken your inner warrior by revisiting the times when you exceeded your expectations. When you won, when you did that amazing overtake or accomplished something due to you being at your best.

Then dissect that great memory and understand how you did it mentally. What you were thinking and feeling.

The memories for awakening and keeping your warrior in control are all accessible and at your mind's fingertips anytime you want them, so use them.

You have met your inner warrior many times. There would have been a time when you stood up to someone or felt mentally on fire, that is your warrior, so rest assured that you have done this many times before.

You have had times when you have proven that you are mentally strong and have the mental skills to overcome adversity, but you need to remind yourself of these moments.

Dust these memories off, bring them to the forefront of your mind and show your warrior these memories and understand how you did it. This will attract your warrior to come forward and be present again.

The more times that you beckon your warrior forward and give them permission to take over the more you will get used to it and reap the rewards that they will get you.

Put simply, this is a case of you getting out of your own way.

You have just shown the warrior what you desperately want to achieve, you have shown them how you may have been underperforming up to now, you have shown them what you don't want to happen and are determined to improve things, that's the hard work of convincing them all done.

Now you need to walk forward and let them take over.

Wake your warrior up each morning (as discussed in chapter 21) and let that person attack your days.

You have a great challenge that you have set out in front of you, it's now time to open your mind and let the real you step forward.

Release your inner warrior into your life and let's get this done once and for all.

PART 3
Training Camp

CHAPTER NINE

Training Camp

> "
>
> *"I hate every minute of training. But I said, don't quit,*
> *suffer now and live the rest of your life as a champion"*
> Muhammad Ali

As the title suggests, this is the part where we roll up our sleeves and start the actual mental training part of the program. Here we will get into the most fundamental and integral mental skills needed if you are to master your mind and outperform your former self.

So far in this book we have taken a good look at where you are and where you are heading, we obviously did this so you can see things for how they really are, to fully understand what needs to be done and how urgent this all is. We have pretty much set the scene for your story and your personal journey.

This was an important step because being honest is another vital ingredient for success, if you are to create the life you want then being self-aware is of extreme importance.

The foundations have now been dug out

You will be glad to hear during the first parts of this book you have already initiated your mental reset process. We are not just trying to change things from the surface level up here, instead we have gone a little deeper and have effectively dug out the foundations that lie beneath the surface. It is from here that we will start to build your Warrior's Mind.

This essential phase is what most people ignore and overlook, which is great news for you because already you are doing this the right way.

Next up, we will start pouring in the mental concrete that will allow you to lay a strong platform from which you can build upon.

All the specific skills that you learn throughout this program (and what you learn elsewhere) will only stick and stand strong if they are built upon a solid platform, that is what this Training Camp is going to give you.

During this part of the program we will start the reconditioning phase of your mind and will install the most vital skills that you will need to succeed.

Overview

As a very quick overview, we are about to train the six following skill sets:

1. Create the warrior's outlook and perspective.
2. Install the beliefs that will serve you most.

3. Learn the success secrets used by the champions before you.
4. Train your emotional control.
5. Free your mind from your past.
6. Overcoming the fears that cause most drivers to fail.

After the Training Camp you will already be armed with some of the most life changing and powerful mental weapons that will help you forge the future you want, both in and out of racing.

You will already be mentally ahead of most people on this planet.

We Live In Two Worlds

Chapter Ten

We Live In Your Worlds

"Reality leaves a lot to the imagination"
John Lennon

Whilst on your racing journey you will have surely had someone ask you "What world are you living in?".

This is something that a member of your family (or someone close) asks you when you're sharing some of your viewpoints that they strongly disagree with. We also hear people asking us this when we tell them about our goals in racing or in life and they feel as though we are being unrealistic. Either way it is often a question people ask when they do not share our thoughts or perspective.

If you are striving to achieve something outside the 'norm' then this type of judgement from others is quite common. People will comment on how deluded you are or they will say that you are living in some kind of dream world.

Even though these kinds of comments may not be nice to hear, it is important to understand what is going on here on a deeper level.

They might not be far from the truth when they refer to you being in a different world.

The Two Worlds

We may share the same external environment as everyone else, but individually we experience and see life in our own way.

Each and every one of us walk the same planet but most of us live in two worlds. There is obviously the real world, the external one where we operate in, then there is our internal world, the one where we operate from.

There are some very distinct differences between your external and internal worlds.

The external world is full of billions of other people with their own objectives and life paths, we all coexist and influence each other as we make our way through our life. There are expectations of how we must behave, act and what we should achieve in this external world.

The internal world however is very different. Here we get to have more control, we get to set the rules and create a perspective that can either help us or bring us down in the real world. This internal world is obviously within our mind, it is where the magic happens.

How you operate in your internal world will determine what life you create and what results you get in the external world.

As a human being you take the information from the outside world through your five senses and then translate it in a way that makes sense to you. It is in this process where you create an alternative reality and this is what we are going to target right now.

This is what Part 3 of the Warrior's Mind is all about. It is how we can best create an internal world that helps you externally.

No matter what is going on externally, you are the one that says what it all means, you are the one who sees it your own way and you are the one who decides how to react to it all.

Believe it or not this personal reality that you have has been largely constructed by you.

The beliefs, the personal rules, opinions and meanings that you have attached to things are the building blocks that have built your internal world and your personal philosophy.

In short, your internal world is your mental coding (mental model) and it is responsible for your overall perspective. You then operate from within the confines of that coding and we all get to see how it plays out in reality.

As you can imagine this is an important area to pay attention to and that is why the Training Camp is all based upon this area.

If you are serious about becoming the best driver you can be and succeeding in your sport, then it's an absolute must that your inner world is set up correctly. It must be aligned with your goals and be set up so you can perform as you want.

It's plain to see that many of the drivers out there are conflicted, they have an inner world that doesn't allow them to perform at their best and they are destined to fail before they even start.

That's what I want to help you avoid. This is the most important part of your mental training and will help you no matter what you do in life.

2 Different Worlds Compared

Let me share with you how I have personally seen this working by giving you some typical examples of two different drivers. These two drivers have very different internal worlds and as a result their external worlds go in different directions.

For this example, let's say that both drivers are 16 years old and are competing in the Formula 4 championship. They are similar in terms of their skill level and outright speed, they have the same kind of racing experience and they both have dreams of reaching Formula 1.

On paper, they seem virtually identical and you would give them a similar chance of success, but internally they are quite different.

First off let's take a look at the mental coding for each driver.

Driver 1 - Joe

Joe's mental coding during the race season was heavily influenced by these five main beliefs:

1. My self-worth is related to my results.
2. My teammate's car is quicker.
3. I hate looking silly in front of others.
4. I am fearful of not being good enough.
5. I always seem to have bad luck.

These are the kinds of opinions that Joe has adopted and in turn they have created a certain mindset and have contributed to his perspective of life and racing.

Driver 2 - Rob

Our second driver, Rob, has a mental model that has been driven by these five main beliefs:

1. Results are just feedback; each loss helps me improve.
2. It's up to me to make my car quick.
3. Other people's opinions are not my reality.
4. I search for the truth; I am not afraid of it.
5. I make my own luck.

I think you can see what I have done here, all these beliefs that Rob has completely counteract the beliefs that Joe has. Same topics, but he has a different way of seeing and translating things.

As a result, Rob has used the kind of building blocks (beliefs) that will help him build a different mindset to Joe.

How This Plays Out

Even though I have only shared five of the beliefs that each driver possesses, I am sure that you have already pictured how things will individually play out over the season for these drivers.

You can imagine what their race weekends would be like, how they coped with challenges, how mentally tough they were, what they were like to work with and what their careers will most likely turn out like.

Just like we did with you in the Destiny Mirror, we could set them off on an imaginary journey to see what happens, but the outcome will be of no surprise to you.

OK you cannot precisely predict what will happen because life has a way of changing your course and in racing, money can help your chances of success, but you can at least say which one, Joe or Rob, is more likely to succeed at what they put their mind to.

I don't actually need to imagine what happens because I have seen this play out for real because this is based off two drivers that I have worked with or witnessed within a team. Here is what happened to Joe and Rob.

Joe

He stepped up a category or two due to having family money but he didn't become a professional driver.

He would often fall out with the teams and never looked like he was enjoying his racing. There always seemed to be something wrong, he blamed everybody and everything else for his lack of form and his teammates would usually dominate him mentally.

This caused him to compete using a defensive mentality so it was as if he was trying not to lose, rather than trying to win. This kind of mindset is the death rattle to any sports person.

Joe will probably carry on racing because it gives him an ego stroke and some significance in life but he won't be fulfilled unless he changes his inner rules (the coding of his inner world).

Rob

Rob on the other hand was a relentless driver. The beliefs and rules that guided him produced a completely different mindset and in turn created better results compared to Joe.

He won many races, he never shied away from a challenge and was always up for a fight.

He had his ups and downs, he had people criticising him and had some huge failures, but he still forged on and triumphed. Teams loved to work with him and he created the kind of career that most people can only dream of.

This is how two drivers who have similar speed behind the wheel can have such different outcomes career wise, and the reason for that all too often comes down to their mental programming.

This may sound unrealistic and far-fetched, but this is what we see all the time in this sport. Even though this is 'Motor' sport, there is still a human element to it, the Joe and Rob example here is what that human element looks like.

You will hear people say things like "You just know a champion when you meet one", heck I say that quite often myself, but it is true. You can just tell by the way they are wired and how they approach things; this is all because they operate from within an internal world that allows this to happen.

Priority No. 1 - Alignment

Your inner environment and mental model of the world is largely responsible for the results you get in all parts of your life, so priority No.1 in this Training Camp is to help you align your mental coding with the task in hand.

It is our objective here to create an internal world that allows you to succeed and to mentally equip you with the tools needed.

I am sure that you can associate with both Joe and Rob, you may share certain beliefs with each of them but we need to make your own set of rules to create the perspective that will serve you best depending on your situation.

For the rest of the Training Camp we will do just that, in the next chapter we will focus on the most vital aspect of the Warrior's Mind and if done correctly this will transform your mental performance.

The Matrix

CHAPTER ELEVEN

The Matrix

> **"**
>
> *"Change yourself to become successful"*
> *Nikki Lauda*

He may be known as a comedian and for making us laugh but when I heard Jim Carrey give his Maharishi International University speech, I became an even bigger fan of his.

He spoke some truths that can only be genuinely preached by someone who has lived a full life and reached their childhood dreams yet has experienced what comes along with that so has also had to delve into his own psyche to help figure things out and deal with what you have to face.

One of his insightful one-liners was *"Our eyes are not viewers, they're also projectors that are running a second story over the picture that we see in front of us"*

You don't need to be a university graduate to understand what he meant here. What happens in life happens, but then we put our own labels on things, we see it in our own way and translate it all in a way that makes sense to us individually. We effectively paint our own picture and our own story over what is actually happening in reality.

Our global beliefs, our values and our experiences in life all come together to create our outlook and that causes us to see life in a certain way.

For example, when a disaster happens like a major terrorist attack, people react in different ways. Some people become angry and this may cause them to retaliate or they even want to join the army to fight back. Whilst others feel sorry for all the victims, they become charitable and want to help in some way. Then you get other people who are fearful and initiate their pre-planned prepping procedure ready for the worst-case scenario.

Let me ask you something, how can one single event in life create so many different reactions?

It's the same when your partner tells you that they no longer love you or that they have found someone else, this also causes different reactions in people.

Some people break down and feel deep sadness for months (if not years) on end. As a result they do not want another relationship or even worse, they no longer trust people so it destroys their future relationships.

Other people will take it personally and want to retaliate and have revenge.

Whilst others will feel sad initially, obviously, but then quickly switch into party mode and start celebrating because they realise that they can now find someone else who will deserve their love this time.

This is totally in line with what was stated in the previous chapter about us living in two worlds, an external world that we share with everyone else and an internal world that resides in our mind.

This internal world is basically our mental model and is responsible for our overall perception.

Our mindset, our emotions, our decisions and our mental health are all heavily influenced by our mental model. Our mental model is how we process what is going on, how we internalise it and how we translate it all into an action, a reaction or just a feeling.

In some ways your mental model is your very own microprocessor. You feed it information (data), it then processes that information and provides an output based on instructions stored in the memory.

Disclaimer: Many people freak out when you compare the human brain to a computer but from time to time you will hear me using the workings of a computer as a way of explaining how the brain works. Rest assured I am not saying that the brain is really like a computer because there are many obvious differences, but boy it makes a good metaphorical example sometimes.

Anyway, back to what I was saying.

Thinking back to the Joe and Rob example, by taking just five of their beliefs from each driver, you can imagine what kind of mental models (perceptions) they created for themselves.

That is why it is so vital for us to build a mental model that serves you, that creates a Warrior's Mind and ultimately takes you closer to what you want. We need to set the game up to win here.

The Matrix

If you are a fan of Wachowskis' 1999 film called The Matrix, then you will have a sense of where I am going to take you next and you will appreciate what I am about to say.

If you need a reminder, then The Matrix film was based around a computer program that the human race lived within (mentally). Humans were actually being farmed. At birth each human was placed into a pod where they would spend their lives whilst in an unconscious state completely unaware of their surroundings.

They were effectively placed into a medically induced coma whilst having their bodies were used as batteries. The energy that their bodies provided was used to power the machines that ran the world at that time.

The architect of the Matrix project had to stimulate the minds of the humans in order to keep them under control and avoid the whole system from crashing. To do this he designed a Neural Interactive Simulation where the humans would mentally live in a simulated reality.

The Matrix was a computer generated dreamworld that was used to make people think that they were living life as normal so they would never realise that they were locked away in a pod. That is Virtual Reality at its best right there.

Some people believe that this is possible and that we are currently living in something fairly similar but I am not going to go down that rabbit hole. For you and me right now, we are going to discover how you can use a similar strategy to help you mentally perform better.

Your Mental Model is your Matrix

If you think about it, your mental model is a lot like the Matrix.

Remember what Jim Carrey said as he described the way we all project our own story over what is happening in front of us. It's as if life is a canvas and individually, we paint it the way we want to see it. What happens in life is nearly irrelevant, it is us humans that get to say how we see it and how we react to it.

So in a lot of ways we too live in our own simulated dreamworld. Just as in the film when the architect created a simulation for the human race, we already do the same. Mentally anyway.

This may sound a bit crazy initially but just take the time again to see how we are all doing this.

You already know full well that humans have achieved amazing feats, they have climbed Everest which is nearly 9 kilometres high, they have invented technology such as the iPhone which transports information from space to your pocket in the blink of an eye, they have built planes like the A380 that weighs 573,000kg. How can something that big and heavy even take off let alone fly at 1,000kph and have a range of over 15,000 kilometres?

Well that's because we are humans and can figure this stuff out.

We have created complex languages, the internet, many cures for diseases, power sources, motor vehicles (which is good for race drivers), navigation systems and the list goes on.

I think you will agree that humans are pretty damn impressive and that there isn't much that we can't do, relatively.

However, due to the way that most of us are raised, most humans are self-governed by our mentality and it is our mental limitations that cause us to individually underachieve compared to what we are capable of. I think you will agree with that.

Even with all this proof of what humans have achieved in the past and are doing so right now around us, if your mental Matrix isn't set up correctly then you will ignore this proof and fail to reach your goals.

If your personal Matrix is built up by beliefs and viewpoints like:

- Nobody in our family has been successful so I won't be.
- I don't believe that I am worthy.
- It is too hard.
- I don't want to dedicate my life to something and run the risk of failing.
- Things just never work for me.

Then if on top of these beliefs you were to consistently remember the times when things didn't work out and you hold on to negative comments that people have said about you in the past, then what kind of Matrix do you think you have built?

What is the likelihood of you getting the most out of yourself and being the driver you need to be?

Even though previous drivers have achieved your racing goals already, so they have shown you that it is possible, if your Matrix is programmed in this way then you will lack belief and the warrior mindset needed to reach your goals.

This is exactly what I mean when I talked about us having two worlds.

In holding those beliefs and fuelling it with negative evidence from your past you will be painting a hopeless, self-belief sapping and demotivating picture in front of your eyes.

You will take in reality via your five senses, but with a defeatist viewpoint you will translate it all using your self-limiting Matrix. Then, it is practically game over.

Believe it or not this happens a lot in racing.

Drivers will put a front on and try to make you believe that they are born champions, but very often when they are put under serious pressure, when they have to deal with a failure, when their rival is breathing down their neck in a race or when they have to go sell to a prospective sponsor, their Matrix can cause them to crumble or hide behind an excuse.

Our external and internal worlds have different limitations and rules, so to get the most out of life then it is important for you to make sure that your internal world, your Matrix, is programmed in a way that aligns you with your goals and allows you to perform at your best.

For the purpose of this book, your Matrix needs to be programmed the same way that a warrior's would be programmed.

To be a leader, to be a warrior, you need to see things differently compared to most other people on the planet. From now on we will refer to your internal world, your mental projection of the real world, as your Matrix and we will refine it so your mind works for you, not against you.

This for me is the most vital step to creating the Warrior's Mind, this is programming yourself to be purpose built for the task at hand just as a warrior needs to be to thrive in battle.

Perspective is key

To show you how important having an effective Matrix is, we are going to quickly look outside of motorsport to Albert Einstein and Steve Jobs.

These two people were warriors within their own field and through their actions they managed to influence how the masses think and live day to day. They caused paradigm shifts and raised the bar in and out of their own industries.

You may not be a fan of the personalities of Einstein and/or Jobs but that is irrelevant for us right now, what we are interested in is how they managed to produce different results compared to most humans before and after them.

These two guys both had mindsets that were not fixed and limited, they had Growth Mindsets that enable them to constantly progress towards their visions. Their viewpoints and way of seeing things were vastly different to the norm.

Both Einstein and Jobs would give us insights into how their minds operated through their captured quotes and by the way they worked. This was all visible from the outside.

Albert Einstein

Albert Einstein gave us an insight when he would say things like - *"Imagination is more important than knowledge. Knowledge is limited. Imagination encircles the world"*.

This was a core belief of Einstein and would contribute to building his Matrix.

It was a belief that he would revolve his career around and it would help him come up with conclusions that many scholars could not.

Einstein demonstrated that if you only work from the knowledge that is already in the textbooks and by what you learn in the lab, then you will just come up with the same conclusions as everyone else. So, on top of all his knowledge he also used his imagination to figure things out.

He used what is called Gedankenexperiment, which translates to 'thought experiment'. It means that he would use his imagination to carry out experiments rather than just in the lab.

This way he could get creative without having to work around real world and technological restrictions.

Einstein's most famous thought experiment was when he was only 16 years old and he imagined physically chasing after a beam of light. That very thought experiment played a memorable role in his development of special relativity.

He was a master at seeing things in his own way compared to other physicists and for having different rules for working things out. This served him well in his career, it helped him devise his theory of relativity and hundreds of his other scientific works. As a result Einstein has heavily influenced us as a human race, not only with our understanding of the universe but his theories can even be seen in paper towels, solar power and laser pens. Amazing right?

He operated from a Matrix, that was set up differently to most, an inner world that was built with an outlandish belief system and as a result he produced different outcomes to most.

Steve Jobs

Steve Jobs may have had a different character to Einstein and had different goals (although they both wanted to ping the universe) but Steve was another person who demonstrated the power of perception and in doing so he achieved different results compared to most experts in his industry.

His Matrix was designed in a way that would baffle and infuriate most people but in saying that, it got the job done.

People who worked with Steve had a phrase that described his mentality, they said that he operated using a **'Reality Distortion Field'**.

This has to be one of the coolest descriptions of someone living in their own world (their own Matrix) that I've heard and it backs up everything we are talking about here.

His Matrix was formed by him having huge expectations of himself and this caused him to consistently push to go further and further. Overall it had worked for him to dream big and have big actions to match, and due to this his belief system would be set up that way, thus creating his Matrix (Elon Musk is a person who also operated in this way).

To keep this up, Steve would automatically distort reality in his own mind to help him remove all external limitations and as a result he was the driving force behind Apple and created products that were of premium quality.

You could see this play out when he would go further than other manufacturers when designing his products.

From the Gorilla glass to the font used, he would be meticulous and relentless in his pursuit for providing special products. He would even make sure that his phones and computers were designed as beautifully on the inside as they were on the outside.

Most manufacturers spent little time on such details because the consumer would never see inside the gadgets but in Steve's world this kind of attention to detail was in the company DNA.

You need to see things differently to have such a high standard for a consumer product but in doing so he led the way.

Steve would also set his workforce virtually impossible tasks and deadlines to stick to. The workers would tell him that they couldn't meet his requirements but due to his Reality Distortion Field he would see everything as possible. He, like many entrepreneurs, never listened to the "It can't be done" voice that others had, instead he would persist and somehow he would usually find a way.

He would scream and shout to get that across to his employees and in doing so he would often change their beliefs of what was possible and remove some of their own self limitations.

Either that or they would leave (or get fired).

Of course, there were many times when they simply couldn't meet his crazy deadlines but his approach would drag more out of both himself and his workforce.

Even though he was ruthless and an absolute pain to work with, he would get results and would astonish all of us each time there was a product launch.

Steve Job's company Apple completely disrupted the computing, the music, the music player and the phone industries.

Before he passed away he was planning to revolutionise the TV and car industries next, we can only imagine what he would have done there.

He was the driving force behind it all and as you read this Apple are still riding the wave that he created all that time ago.

If you have a vision and you are determined for that vision to be your reality one day then you need to be a true leader.

True leaders are resourceful, they come up with solutions whilst others think something is impossible, they are relentless, obsessed, have unrealistic expectations and dare to think big.

The thing that people would criticise Steve for and call his Reality Distortion Field, was what his Matrix created. It was the way he viewed the world and it served him best, the Matrix he operated from helped him achieve what most didn't think was possible.

Geniuses are crazy

We label people as geniuses when they are outstanding in their respective field, when they defy public belief and raise the bar within their professional community.

What you will also notice is that society often labels these geniuses as eccentric or slightly crazy or "wired differently".

Individuals like Muhammad Ali, Richard Branson, David Goggins, Serena Williams, Michael Jordan, Oscar Wilde, Jim Carrey, John McEnroe, Michael Phelps, Howard Hughes and Mike Tyson.

People in motorsport who fit this description are Colin McRae, Travis Pastrana, Ayrton Senna, Nigel Mansell, Dale Earnhardt, Enzo Ferrari, Nikki Lauda and Michael Schumacher.

These are just to name a few but they are all human beings who are regarded as geniuses in some way and they are people who had something different about them. Their persona, their actions and the way they operated caused them to create outstanding results.

They were either obsessive, quirky or people would say that they were downright crazy.

If one of these individuals was to walk in the room right now you would just sense that they were different in some way. If you worked with them then it would be a challenge to keep up and if you competed against them then you would have a serious fight on your hands. All previous rules would go out the window because they operated using a different set of inner rules.

Some of these individuals were not the best at handling their behaviour or emotions (we will address this later in the Training Camp) but they were undeniably purpose built for the task in hand. They possessed a mindset that enabled them to deliver impressive performances time and time again.

There is a lesson here because our desire for being liked and loved by all is a major performance blocker that humans have. We are not here to piss people off but just know that when you perform at your best, when you fully express yourself whilst competing and let yourself go, it can rub others up the wrong way. But you need to do that to get the most from yourself. You must freely express yourself whilst competing without worrying too much about others.

So for being a person who is dedicated to their craft and creating the mindset needed to succeed then you will ruffle a few feathers along the way. The feathers of people who are underachieving and maybe even jealous of your success.

That is one of the reasons why so many super successful people create haters to start with, but then over time these haters become their biggest fans. You must be prepared for this.

Your World

I hope that I have gotten across the importance of creating your own reality, of giving yourself a purpose-built perspective on life that causes you to see things in a way that helps you perform at a higher level.

This is all about warping reality so that your mind works with you rather than against you, it raises your own personal limitations and puts higher benchmarks in place.

This doesn't mean that you must believe in fairy tales or be in denial about reality, because that would be outright delusion and will get you nowhere. You are just moulding your mind so it translates the external world in a way that serves you and your quest to your North Star.

To put it another way, you are creating your own realm, your own internal world, your own kingdom...your own Matrix.

In your Matrix you get to set the rules, you get to choose what things mean and what beliefs form its framework.

You are the lord almighty of your own Matrix, the architect, and you are the one who sets things up to create your warrior mind.

How to build a new Matrix

Now that you are clear on what is meant by your Matrix and you are probably thinking "Ok Enzo, I get it", then naturally I need to tell you how you go about creating a new one of your own.

Whilst on your racing quest, you are the warrior that is battling your way forward and the leader of your assault, for you to succeed you need to have the kind of internal coding that will give you a good shot at this.

Like any computer that is purpose built, the coding installed sets up how it will act, react and the rules that it operates by. If you change a part of its coding or if it has certain conflicts within its operating system, then it will not work properly... it is the same for you.

We need to iron out any glitches, we need to cleanse you of as many internal conflicts as possible and we need to delete the coding that does not serve you.

If we do this then we will create the Warrior's Mind.

Before we do anything, we need to get clear on what elements come together to form your Matrix, then for the rest of the Training Camp we will condition and improve these elements.

We have already started

You will be glad to hear that we have already started to build your new and improved Matrix, we did this in the previous part of this book.

The foundations that you set in Your Awakening helped you see what is going on in your life and helped direct your focus on what needs to happen internally. All of this is a necessary first stage when creating a new mindset and outlook on life.

If you want to change a behaviour, improve your beliefs, or disrupt a habit that you have, then you need to shock the brain out of its automatic procedures and interrupt its viewpoint. Put simply, if you want to change something about yourself mentally then you need to effectively slap your current mind in the face and give it a reality check that shows what will happen if it carries on doing what it is doing.

Your mind also needs to be shown the benefits it will receive and that it can meet its true goals if it changes its way.

Teaching your mind a new way of behaving is just like teaching a child or a pet dog how to behave a certain way. We use the Pain and Pleasure principle to learn a better way to operate. That is what the Destiny Mirror was all about.

When you see that your behaviour is having a detrimental impact on your life and your results, and you really allow it to hit home and sink in, then your mind creates the motivation to change.

This is an essential step when you are trying to change anything about yourself. Particularly when you are attempting to change your overall mindset.

On top of that you also now know the importance of creating your Matrix in the first place, again this is another important part of the building phase, knowing what you are going to accomplish from this.

With all this knowledge and information you have now formed a strong platform from which you can build up from.

What builds your Matrix

Your Matrix has many contributing factors, we will call these the **Building Materials**. They all come together to build your overall mentality and they form the framework of your Matrix.

So if you are looking to modify the way your mind works then the best thing to do is to find out what is currently influencing it.

There are many things that contribute to and influence your inner environment, and the perspective you have, but I have simplified it down to six elements that are taught in many psychology sciences and therapies today.

Here are six of the main building materials that come together to build your Matrix:

1. Your Values
2. Your Rules
3. Your Beliefs
4. Your Knowledge
5. Your Past
6. Your Influences

We will spend the Training Camp improving and enhancing all six of these, one by one, so by the time you have finished this part of the book you will be well on your way to improving your mind.

Each building material will have its own chapter followed by its own training exercise.

Building Material No.1 – Your Values

CHAPTER TWELVE

Building Material No.1 – Your Values

> *"It's not hard to make decisions once you know what your values are"*
>
> Roy E. Disney

If you have been into personal development and mental training for some time then you will have heard a lot about values. Values are near the top of what humans live and are prepared to die for, they are the certain things in life that your mind prioritises and pays attention to.

Our minds are being fed so much information from the outside world via our senses and if we were to pay attention to all of that information then we would quickly become overwhelmed and ready to burst.

Your mind sifts through all that external data is to prioritise what's important to it, the kind of things that it values most. These are obviously known as our values.

We have two types of values:

1. **Target Values** - The things, feelings, emotions and experiences that we want.

2. **Avoidance Values** - The things, feelings, emotions and experiences that we want don't want.

When it comes to your Matrix it is important to know what your mind is searching for and what it is trying to avoid because these values are related to your overall mindset and heavily affect your mental performance both in and out of the car.

If you know what somebody values, then you get an insight of what they want and don't want in life. Then beyond that, if you know how they plan to attain the things they value, then you can predict their behaviour.

But we are not here to elicit other people's values just yet, today we are solely focused on you.

Target Values

When working with drivers it is important for me to understand early on what drives them, what values they want and how they go about attaining them.

If I ask them straight out "What are the things you value in life?" or "What are you in racing for?" (these are the types of questions you ask someone when trying to elicit their values), then they often tell me things like:

- Winning

- Money
- Danger
- Being number one
- Fame
- The thrill of being wheel to wheel

If you just take a look at these values alone and just imagine that one driver told me that these were the things they were after, then I think you'd get a sense of what this person is like.

Ok you will not know everything about their personality because that would depend on how they go about fulfilling these values (that's Building Material No.2), but you will certainly know what that person is aiming for and what they spend their time thinking about.

This is like a subconscious shopping list that our minds have.

From all the information coming in from the outside world your brain filters it all looking for the things that you value, and ignores the things that are of no interest to it. You will have an internal pull towards these values which will compel you to do things to get them and will influence you to design your life so you experience them regularly.

At some point your mind figured out that it could fulfil most of its values through motorsport and because of that it has formed a love for the sport. It is one of the main activities that allows you to fully express yourself and where you can get what you want out of life. From the moment you realised this, your mind started to prioritise everything that is related to motorsport and before you know it your Instagram feed is full of everything racing. That is why your values are a super important building material for your Matrix.

Surface Values = Core Values

I want you to understand that these values I have just listed out (winning, money, danger, etc) are only surface values. A driver will only value winning because of what winning will provide him or her emotionally.

Drivers will want money because of what money provides them emotionally not because they want pieces of paper or digits on a computer screen.

Drivers will only value danger because of how that will make them feel.

So there are two levels to the values that you are seeking, they are your surface values and your core values. Your surface Values are the vehicles that deliver the core values that you really desire.

To put this in another popular way, **our surface values are just a means to an end. Our core values are the end**.

Everything we want externally is driven by an internal desire and that internal desire is usually an emotion or something that we feel we need in our lives.

If we take some of the values that race drivers had from that list, and translate those values into what the drivers were really after (their core values), then it would look something like this:

Winning = respect, confidence, love and pride.

Money = security, freedom, variety and significance.

The Thrill = adventure, excitement, spontaneity and challenge.

Fame = significance, purpose, power and influence.

There are many other core values that some of these surface values provide us with, like our ability to contribute to others, our sense of achievement, having a feeling of progress...and so on but I think you get the idea.

The core values that are mentioned here are the kind that most of us share and we go through life looking for ways to get them.

Avoidance Values

As well as the things that your mind is constantly seeking to obtain, you also have certain values that you desperately want to avoid.

These are the types of emotions and feelings that you don't like and your mind is looking out for these so it can protect you from them.

Once again, over the years when I have asked drivers what they don't want, they will tell me values they want to avoid like:

- Losing
- Being slow
- Getting dropped
- Running out of money

- Crashing

As you can tell, these fears are just surface values. If we were to dig a little deeper and understand what they really mean to a driver on an emotional level then you start to understand the core Avoidance Values that a particular driver has.

Like before we can translate parts of the list to expose the core Avoidance Values. It would look something like this.

Losing = frustration, embarrassment or loss of respect.

Getting dropped = rejection, worry or depression.

Crashing = regret, remorse or anger.

Some of the so-called 'failures' that drivers experience are directly linked to some of the core values that they want to avoid most. That is why it is so painful when experiencing them.

Drivers may be seen as superheroes but usually you will find that they want to avoid the very same emotions and feelings that most people do.

Some of the biggest fears that people have and values they want to avoid are loss of love and feeling inadequate. For a human to feel like they are not enough is a cause for serious pain, same for race drivers.

Remember how this plays out

If you think back to the examples of the drivers Joe and Rob, and how their outlooks influenced their life paths, this is what you will see when it comes to values.

In fact this can be said for each of the six building materials that we will go through, they all contribute to producing a mindset and a personality of a person.

For values alone, can you imagine the difference in what a person thinks about and how they may act in daily life if we had these two people with these two different sets of values.

Person A

Person A has the following surface and core values that drive them.

Target Values:

- Fame
- Significance
- Winning
- Money
- Image
- Power

Avoidance Values:

- Compassion
- Charity

- Security
- Health
- Connection with others
- Community

I think by just looking at these values, you can kind of get a sense of what this person is like, what they pay attention to and even the kinds of goals they may have.

Person B

Person B's values are the following.

Target Values:

- Compassion
- Charity
- Security
- Health
- Connection with others
- Community

Avoidance Values:

- Fame
- Significance
- Winning
- Money
- Image
- Power

You can see what I did here.

That was not to be lazy or to catch you out, I did this to demonstrate how the same values, being shuffled around, will create a different type of mindset. If one person avoids what someone else targets, then you get two people who have completely opposite priorities in life.

Looking at these two people you can get a sense for how their kind of internal coding can impact their Matrix.

They would go for different jobs, set up their lives in a way where their values were being met and even have different personalities.

Peron A is more likely to be some daredevil who is filming themselves base jumping to get a few more Instagram followers.

Whereas Person B is more likely to be a person who may choose to work for charity in Ghana.

Beware of conflicts

We have to be mindful of certain conflicts within our values.

If you desperately want to **succeed** and you know that this is an important Target Value for you, yet you also have **failure** and **rejection** as important Avoidance Values, then you may be conflicted.

When I say conflicted I mean that you have important values on each side that pull against each other and cause you to feel stuck or to hesitate. This is a mental tug of war that a lot of people suffer with.

You may want to go and speak to that potential sponsor across the room because they could help you **succeed** by sponsoring you, but due to your fear of **failure** and **rejection** you may talk yourself out of approaching them.

That is an examples of how your mind uses 'pain and pleasure' to make decisions. This is where the 'wiring' of your mind can make it hard for you to succeed.

You will only approach that potential sponsor if the pleasure of getting sponsorship outweighs the pain of being told to "Get lost". That's how your mind makes decisions, it weighs things up first and your values are a big part of this decision process.

Your mind wants to protect you so usually drivers will chicken out when in this situation, so be careful of this.

When you have this kind of internal programming, you may come up with an excuse like "Uh, it might not be a good time for them" or "I don't think I have my pitch down perfectly yet, so I'll wait until next time".

You see people and drivers doing this kind of thing all the time.

I am sure that you are starting to see the importance of how your values MUST be the kind of values that virtually force you to take action, that compel you to be the person you need to be in order to get the job done. In short, you need your values to be the kind that a warrior would have.

Failure and rejection will naturally be on your Avoidance Value list, but we have to make sure that they are not a priority and are lower down the list because you know that you have to fail a few times before you succeed.

Values of a Warrior's Mind

What I am about to say is not completely accurate but just for the purposes of this example, these are typical values that a Warrior's Mind would possess.

Target Values:

- Personal growth
- Purpose
- Love / passion
- Self-expression
- Integrity
- Leadership

Avoidance Values:

- Laziness
- Regression
- Negativity
- Unjust
- Quitting
- Indecisiveness

This is a very templated look at some of the values, they will differ from warrior to warrior but when you meet a champion in a sport, you will find these kinds of values in place. They are the values that build a Matrix that urges a person to step up and fight for something that is bigger than just themselves.

Someone with this internal coding will have a desire to improve themselves and constantly move forward. They will make sure that they work tirelessly each day and will give everything they have no matter how others may judge them.

When you are fighting against someone like this in motorsport then you have a one tough opponent to deal with, they will just keep coming at you no matter what you throw at them.

I want this someone to be you.

Values in a nutshell

To give you an overview, just remember the types of values:

Target Values - Surface and Core Values that you want.

Avoidance Values - Surface and Core Values that you want to avoid.

Due to your mind using pain and pleasure as a motivator and as something to help us make decisions, it will attach pleasure to the things that we want (our Target Values) and it will attach pain to the things that we don't want (our Avoidance Values).

We navigate through life using our values as our internal compass.

Next, we will do our first training exercise and find out your values.

Training Exercise – Your Values

Before you forget, this part of the book is called Training Camp, not study camp, so now is the time for you to take on what we have covered here and to start to change your mental coding to create the Matrix that will serve you best.

Changing your thinking and improving your mental performance can be seen in a similar way to when we reprogram an AI robot.

If we wanted to change the purpose or make an AI work better, then we would edit the coding within its computer brain. We would go in, do a bit of coding, and then see how it performs.

That is pretty much what we are doing here.

Ok 'reprogramming' the human brain is a pipe dream because we need to constantly condition our minds to change its behaviour long term but essentially we are changing its coding and designing your mind to help you rather than hinder you.

This will be constant work in progress but if you treat your mind as if it were a muscle and understand that it requires consistent conditioning to keep it strong and purposeful, then you will see that it is possible to enhance your operating system so it serves you and helps you perform at a higher level.

The first part of the coding change will be within your values. We need to make sure that your values are aligned with the person you need to become.

I will now take you through an exercise that will help you do that.

What you will need

To do most of the training exercises, including this one, you will again need the Warrior's Mind Workbook from our website, so get that to hand if you can.

You will also need to be in an environment where you can be free from interruption and distraction. Give this your full attention, your mind deserves it.

Some of the exercises may require you to close your eyes so please no doing this as you are driving or doing anything else that requires your attention.

Step 1 - Elicit Your Current Values

We need to get clear on what your mind has been focusing on over recent months.

The kind of things it values and what it is paying attention to. This will show you how your mind is navigating through the world at the moment as it seeks for what it wants and for what it's trying to avoid.

To kick this off I want you to list out what has been important to you, the 5 or 6 things that you have been valuing most.

Once you know this then you can see a couple of things, firstly you will notice if you have been meeting these values and needs that you have.

If you have not been meeting your Target Values on a consistent basis then this will explain why you may have been feeling down, had lack of confidence or motivation, or feel stuck and frustrated. That is usually because you are not feeling the emotions that you came to this sport for in the first place, so it doesn't feel good.

Consider this as your signal that something must change as soon as possible.

The second thing that this exercise will allow you to do is to see if your values are actually aligned with your goals.

Question 1

To help you out, I am going to ask you a question that will help you pinpoint your values. When answering this I want you to think of the things that you value about the sport, the things you want (your Target Values).

To help find out what is driving you, answer these two questions:

What is important to me in racing?

Why do I want to succeed, what will it give me?

To elaborate on this, what things must you experience for you to be happy in racing?

Write out all the single things you will get from succeeding as a race driver and list them out. Create your short list by either writing the answers on a piece of paper or use the designated area in your WM Workbook.

To inspire you, here is a list of common Target Values that people have and what they are after by achieving their goals.

Common Target Values:

- Acceptance
- Achievement
- Adventure
- Ambition
- Brave
- Calm
- Certainty
- Commitment
- Confidence
- Contribution
- Courageousness
- Creativity
- Decisiveness
- Energy
- Excitement
- Focus
- Freedom
- Gratefulness
- Growth
- Happiness
- Honesty
- Kindness
- Learning
- Love
- Optimism
- Passion

- Positivity
- Power
- Progress
- Purpose
- Security
- Significance
- Spontaneity
- Success
- Stability

Question 2 - What order are your values in?

It's quite obvious to say that you will have favourable values, you will value some more than others.

Put your values in order so you can start to see what your mind is trying to achieve most and begin to understand what it prioritises as it goes through life. This can be interesting.

Do that now.

Question 3 - What are the things you desperately want to avoid in racing?

It's time to do the same for your Avoidance Values. In your racing world, what are the things you most want to avoid happening or feeling?

What emotions do you hate living with?

Again there is an example list here to inspire you but feel free to add your own.

Common Avoidance Values:

- Abandonment
- Anger
- Anxiety
- Conflict
- Deception
- Depression
- Dishonesty
- Embarrassment
- Failure
- Hopelessness
- Humiliation
- Hurt
- Indecisiveness
- Insecurity
- Jealousy
- Loneliness
- Loss
- Nervousness
- Regret
- Rejection
- Resent
- Sadness
- Shame

- Stress
- Unloved
- Weak
- Worthlessness

Which things hurt you the most? Think back to the emotions you felt when you were feeling low over recent times and you will have your answers for this.

Question 4 - What order are your Avoidance Values in?

Next, put these values in order of importance. Which ones do you want to avoid most?

There will be certain Avoidance Values that you fear or dislike most, put them at the top of your short list.

Have you been meeting your values?

Thank you for answering the previous questions, these will help you understand the top end of your coding and will help you going forward.

If you think back to your Destiny Mirror and the timeline within it, it can be useful to look at your values to understand why you may have been feeling down or unfulfilled at times.

You may not be getting the results you want or feel up for it because you are being starved of the things you mentally crave in life. Plus, you might feel as though you are exposed to your Avoidance Values.

When you look back like this you can start to become clear on things and just understand a little bit more about yourself.

Step 2 - Look for high priority conflicting values

As you look at your values lists, both target and avoidance, can you see any priority values that may be causing conflicts?

For example, if **success** is something that you have high up in your Target Values, but you also have **failure** high up in your Avoidance Values then this can cause a conflict.

It can cause a mental tug of war between something you know you should do, but you can't get yourself to do it. This is a common trap that people set up for themselves.

You are obviously going to have to fail quite a few times before you get it right, it's part of the learning process. So I don't want you to be scared of taking the required actions.

When you have the kind of coding that has success and failure at the top of each list then it can cause you to feel stuck and it creates anxiety when it is your time to shine.

Exception to that rule

As with every rule, there is always an exception. If you have failure high up in your Avoidance Values list and you like it there because it motivates you, then that's OK.

That means you have altered what failure means to you and you are using it as a motivational strategy.

We will get into that in the next chapters when we talk about your rules and beliefs around achieving your values.

In the short term this strategy can work well but over time you will get tired of the threat and it should naturally sink down the list.

I want you to only highlight and notice values that are conflicting and as a result may cause you to underperform.

Step 3 - Create the value lists of a warrior

As you look at those values and think about the ways in which you attain them, are they the type of values that a warrior would have?

Are they the value lists that would guide your actions and create the necessary behaviours of someone who could blast their way to your North Star in record time?

If they are then perfect, you already have the correct coding here and you can move on.

If not, then I want you to start to look at the ones that are no longer helping you, that are causing you to be too quiet in the industry, that are not allowing you to go full out and be the person you want to be. Then it's time to discard them.

For example if you have Target Values...

- Significance

- Fame
- Money
- Getting ahead

...as your top values, then this may be ok for a while but these are also the kinds of values of a conman. These could well create behaviour that causes you to only think of you, to use people and to be selfish.

This sport is too small and you need many people to join you if you are going to make it.

So if you start using people and casting them aside when you think they are no longer of use, so all your relationships are one way, then word will get out about this and eventually you will end up being left in the dark.

If you want to really increase your chances of success and have a warrior's kind of value system then it would look more like this:

- Contribution
- Personal growth
- Collective progress
- Team

These are the kind of values to have if you want to build your own success army, the people who you can join and collectively provide each other with value.

This is a reminder of just how important your values are when it comes to creating your behaviour.

Play around

By all means you can have different values for different parts of your life. You will have different values in your career than you will in your personal relationships.

Values are just the things that you believe you need to be in place in order for you to be happy or sad, so set these rules up to help you feel what you want to feel and at the same time they allow you to achieve the outcomes that you want.

You don't need to get this right first time, play with them and see the effects.

Figuring out your values and finding out what works for you is part of growing up and maturing, you will change them over time and tailor them to your situation.

Building Material No.2 – Your Rules

CHAPTER THIRTEEN

Building Materials No. 2 – Your Rules

> **"**
>
> *"Make your own rules or be a slave to another man's"*
> *William Blake*

Now that you have gotten clear on your values and you know what your mind is constantly on the hunt for, next we will discover how this really shapes your behavior and how it can either make or break your racing career.

To discover this we need to go one level deeper into your Matrix and take a look at some of your guiding beliefs.

You will have developed conclusions for how best to attain your Target Values at the same time as staying arms-length away from its Avoidance Values.

We will call these conclusions, your Rules.

We will delve into other beliefs in the next chapter but for now your rules are the top beliefs you have for meeting your values.

What rules look like

Everybody on this planet has attached rules to each of their values. Here is how a rule may look.

If a driver's main reason for being in racing was to make themselves significant in their sport (if their priority Target Value was Significance), then they may have a subconscious rule for achieving that value which goes something like this:

"For me to feel significant, I need people to tell me that I am the best driver on the grid".

This one rule would most likely cause that driver to crave the praise from others. If other people were to say good things about them then that driver would feel happy.

However, if others were to verbally criticise that driver then they would feel less worthy and it may harm their confidence.

This one rule can shape that driver's behaviour and influence how easily they are affected by what others think. This is such a common problem.

Just by looking at this rule I am sure that you can imagine how poorly this driver would handle negative comments about them on social media or how frustrated they would get when people get the wrong idea about them.

This driver's emotions and state of mind would be inconsistent due to them having too much ego wrapped up in what other people say and this will make them vulnerable.

Just so you know, this is the opposite to what a warrior's rule would be.

You will also have a plan for achieving each rule

Underneath each rule we have plans in place for attaining them.

Going back to our example driver who wants to be told that they are the best so they can feel significant, they could choose any one of these five plans to help that achieve this:

1. I must dominate the championship so it is undeniable and clear for people to see that I am the best.
2. If my teammate is quick then I will play mind games to put them off their game.
3. I will constantly tell everyone that I am the best.
4. I will prove it on the track, if it is said by people then I know I have made it.
5. If I am quicker than my teammates on the data, then I will make sure the whole team knows about it.

As you read these plans for how certain drivers approach getting significance, I am sure that you can see what different characters and personalities these plans could cause.

Plans No. 1 and No. 4 are more based on results. A driver with these plans will still crave the compliments from other people, but they want to have it because of what they do on track. They want people to conclude things on their own and then communicate it to them verbally.

A driver who uses plan No. 2 will try and bring his teammates and others down in order to get the edge over them.

Whereas a driver with plans No. 3 and No. 5, will tell everyone how good they are in the hope that others will believe them.

As an individual you can have the same values as someone else, you may even have the same rule as them, but if your plan for attaining that rule differs then you can get a completely different person.

This is mental coding

This is what you call the coding of the mind and it is important to understand if your coding is helping you or not.

It is in this area where we set up the game to win by aligning your values, rules and plans with the goals that you have. We must make sure that all of this serves you and helps you advance.

As with emotions, I like to see all of this as an equation where you add things together and get an outcome.

The equation on this subject would look like this:

Plan + Rule + Value = Result

Or as a process:

Plan → Rule → Value → Result

Apart from your driving skills, your results and performance are heavily affected by your values, the rules you have about attaining your values, and the plan you have for achieving those rules.

It determines where your focus goes, where your time is spent and it forms your overall strategy in racing.

As a result, all of this coding is partially responsible for your behaviour, your reactions to when you are challenged, your reactions to when things do not go to plan, your mental health, your mindset, your reputation in the sport, your attitude and your overall chances of success. It really is that important.

Race Drivers and Serial Killers

To give you an extreme example, I want to ask you a few questions.

What do you think separates a race driver from a serial killer?

Is it their upbringing?

Is it the things that have happened to them as a child?

Is it just a case of a serial killer having a mental disorder that causes them to commit such crimes when a race driver wouldn't even dream of doing the things they do?

Any of these (or all of these) reasons may contribute to why they do what they do but at the end of the day a serial killer comes up with certain rules and plans that make sense to them and helps them meet their values.

Believe it or not, race drivers are quite similar to serial killers.

There is a thin line between someone who races around at track and someone who attempts to end the lives of others.

Ok when it comes to serial killers there will be other factors that come into play but this is just my way of giving you an extreme example to help explain how our minds are set up and it all causes us to act in certain ways.

I don't know what you put on your values list but if you were to have the following as being your priority Target Values in motorsport...

- Excitement
- Progress
- Significance
- Spontaneity
- Respect
- Adventure

...then you may be surprised to learn that a serial killer might just share the same values as you.

As a race driver, the values of Significance and Respect usually mean a lot to you.

At some point your mind came up with the belief that it can gain those values by winning, and to do this in the sport that you love so much would be heaven to you.

Your mind will have developed a plan (a guiding belief) that goes something like this..."*If I win the championship, then I will feel fulfilled because I will experience Significance in life and will have Respect from those in the industry.*"

It may even visualize the long game and give even more emphasis on winning the title by believing... *"If I win the championship then this will open up doors of so I can Progress to the next formula and experience even more Significance and Respect".*

Once you start to stack things like this then it all becomes even more ingrained in your mind (I put in the value called Progress which is another common Target Value).

That my friend is the mind becoming addicted to something.

Once you conclude that you can meet your highest values by doing a certain activity, then you become obsessed with it. Plus, if at the same time it takes you away from your Avoidance Values then you will be in love with that activity.

That activity will become your passion.

Back to our serial killer. They may also be hunting for Significance and Respect, but somewhere along the way they didn't take up racing or any other sport, instead they concluded that they can do this by harming others.

At some point they would have developed a guiding belief that goes something like... *"If I go out and end the life of that person, for that moment I will be Significant to them, they will notice me and I will be in Control. Heck even if I get caught then it's still a plus because they may even make a Netflix documentary about me"*

I slipped in yet another value called Control then because it fitted well and it is actually another value that many top drivers have.

A serial killer may also be driven by revenge on certain types of people (because of something that may have happened to them earlier in life) but still, they will simply be hunting for what they value and then obey the inner rules and plans that make sense to them.

They too will be meeting the other values on that list like Excitement, Spontaneity, Adventure, etc. Even if they had Progress as something that is important to them then they would meet that in some way, maybe by the number of people they have attacked, by how good they were getting at it or by how much risk they can take without getting caught.

Before they know it, harming others becomes their viable cause of action for them to get their fix.

This all may sound sick and twisted but the Matrix of a murderer goes a long way to answering why they choose to harm others. Once you start to understand how the mind's coding is responsible for its behaviour then you can start to understand why people do what they do, no matter how extreme their behaviour is.

It also hits home how important this is for you if you want to behave differently to how you have been up to now.

This can be said for many people who also could share this same list of values, like those who take part in Wingsuit flying, actors, singers and even drug dealers.

Many people who take part in activities like these are also doing it to meet the same values of adventure, excitement, significance, spontaneity and respect.

On the opposite side to this, if you were to find somebody who was to be driven by Target Values like...

- Calmness
- Security
- Peace
- Safety

...plus they possessed Avoidance Values like...

- Failure
- Physical harm
- Embarrassment
- Risk

...then most likely they wouldn't be the type of person who would risk jumping off cliffs in Wingsuits, racing cars or singing on stage.

Some rules and plans

To bring things back to racing and away from murderers, it goes without saying that we are virtually on autopilot being run by our Matrix and the coding that builds it.

Over the years you get to see what this looks like as you work with drivers. You see how all these drivers share the same values as each other but they go about attaining them in different ways.

Let's take a look at the value called Respect.

I can immediately think of three drivers who all had Respect as a major Target Value.

When it came to them figuring out how they would get that respect within their race teams, all three of them came up with a different way for doing so.

Here are their personal rules and plans:

Driver No.1 believed... *"I will know when I have won the respect of my team when they see me as the model driver. To do that I will always be on time and do what the team wants"*

Driver No.2 believed... *"I will know when I have won the respect of my team when they regard me as one of the fastest drivers they have ever worked with. To do that I will be more prepared than anyone else, I will make sure that I am always fast and will win in their car"*

Driver No.3 believed... *"I will know when I have won the respect of my team when they like me. To do that I will always get along with everyone and be their friend"*

Three drivers with three different beliefs, causing three different behaviours. These would cause the drivers to apply themselves and approach their race weekends in different ways.

Driver No.1 was prioritising their duties by being first to fill out their driver feedback reports, by being first to the track and keeping their work area clean.

Driver No.2 was less worried about their punctuality and housekeeping tasks, instead they put all of their effort into their driving and performance. They prepared well, continued to dissect their data by themselves even after their debrief session with their engineer, they prioritised personal development and went heavily into understanding the car setup.

Whereas driver No.3, well, you would often find him joking around. He would be showing the mechanics his funny pics on his phone and will be chatting a lot to the team members.

What was interesting about Driver No.3 was that when he saw his teammates working hard, he would not work hard to compete with them, instead he would become louder and double down on his chosen plan. This shows much he believed in it.

Even though he started to annoy the team and they didn't take him seriously, he failed to have the self-awareness to notice this and instead of seeing it and adjusting his behaviour, he continued to stick to his subconscious strategy.

Sometimes our rules and plans don't even make sense when we take a proper look at them.

Become a Master Translator

There will be a lot of translation skills that you must master during the Warrior's Mind and your values are the first thing I want you to get good at translating.

I say this because there will be many ways in which you can achieve your values, but we must make sure that you do it in a way that helps you most and does not hamper your performance or your reputation in the sport.

If you want to succeed then your beliefs around your values must serve you and help you get the most out of your one shot in racing.

Driver No.3 from the recent example was so obsessed with being liked, that it took his eye off the ball performance-wise, so he constantly under-performed.

His attention was more about being one of the boys rather than the fastest he could be. That is first-hand evidence that the beliefs you have heavily influence the success you will experience.

I want you to translate your values in the best way possible, to take another look at your values and come up with a set of strategies that will best help you globally.

Your Warrior Code

When you start to look at your values and create the best ways for attaining them you start to come up with your own Warrior Code.

This is like a code of conduct that you stand by and use to keep you behaving as you need to so you can stay on track. By listing out your values and beliefs around them in this way, you are forming your own success code and philosophy.

You don't need to worry about putting your dedicated Warrior Code together just yet, for now just know that during this part of the book you will be contributing to it and planting seeds within your mind that will help you come up with your own code.

Being on autopilot with that kind of internal coding will help you massively.

In your training exercise for this chapter I will talk you through the rules and plans that will help you advance from here on out.

Training Exercise – Your Rules

To start the process of building both your Matrix and to start the creation of your own Warrior Code, we will do the following:

First - Pick the top core Target Values that you have for your racing. The things that you really want out of racing and will cause you to feel fulfilled.

Second - Come up with a rule for each value. Understand what needs to be in place for you to feel that value (emotion or feeling).

Third - Create a plan that will help you get it in the most productive way.

Example

I will give you an example of what this may look like.

Let's say that you have **Significance** as one of your main Targets Values, then you will have a rule that tells you when you have achieved it.

A rule usually takes the form of sentences that are configured with *"If ___ then___"* or *"To feel___ I must___"*.

So for this example you may have a set rule that you think about in the following way/s:

- **"If people know my name when I walk into a room, then I will feel significant"**
- **"To feel significant, I must be known by everyone in the industry".**

This is you creating a personal rule (a belief) for significance that not only suggests the standard that you operate by but you are also stating when you are allowing yourself to feel significant. A rule that tells you when you have met that value.

If you had a few days when you didn't feel this emotion and was feeling ignored by the industry, then you would feel unfulfilled and will have something missing in life.

This is simply a rule that you create and your mind then follows it as gospel.

Then underneath each rule you will have a plan in place for how you will achieve it. It may look something like this:

My Target Value: Significance.

My Rule: If people know my name when I walk in the room, then I will feel significant.

My Plan: I will post on social media every day. I will make sure that my website is always updated. My helmet colour must be bright and I must stand out when on track. I will do a lot of interviews on podcasts and in general media. I must win on track and make sure that I am with the best teams possible.

And so on.

So you have the Target Value, the rule that tells you when you have achieved it, and the plan for how to achieve it.

You can do this for your Avoidance Values

If you wish, you can also do the same for your Avoidance Values.

That may look something like this:

My Avoidance Value: Failure.

My Rule: If I try but easily give up on something, then I will have failed.

My Plan: I will never give up on the things that matter to me. If something doesn't work out then I will change my process and try again. I will continue to do this over and over until I get the result I want.

That's the plan to have to avoid failure. This is you changing your rules for when you allow yourself to feel like a failure. When you do this you can often find that you go from having Failure as a top Avoidance Value, and due to your new way of seeing things it slips down the priority list.

You will always have failure on your Avoidance List somewhere because it can drive you and you don't want to end up there, but your beliefs around failure need to serve you, not cause you to freeze. I know, I am repeating myself, I do that a lot for the things that I want to get across.

Perfection is not the goal here

You don't have to get this completely correct the first time you do this, it is your first stab at it and over the next weeks, months and years you will keep adjusting your beliefs as you go.

Your priorities will naturally change as you age as you take on all kinds of different goals. First you need to test drive this new focus and rules in life to see if they work for you and if they improve your mindset.

For now, the exercise is to go to the MW Workbook and start to write out your top values, the rules you have for them and the best plans possible for attaining them.

These are going to be the strategies that you live by going forward and will help you succeed. This is the creation of your Warrior Code and how you will conduct yourself.

Building Material No.3 – Your Beliefs

CHAPTER FOURTEEN

Building Materials No. 3 – Your Beliefs

> ❝
>
> *"Whether you think you can or you think you can't – you*
>
> *are right"*
>
> *Henry Ford*

In this chapter I want to focus solely on the important area of your beliefs, the different types of beliefs that are most relevant to you as a person who is attempting to become a champion in their sport.

Just like you did with language, we pick up our values and beliefs as we go through life. First our parents subjected us to their way of seeing the world and we took on some of the values and beliefs that they taught us. They taught us how to behave, what to do and what not to do. All based on their personal opinions.

Then after that initial period we went to school and took on more values and beliefs that we picked up from our friends and teachers.

Some of which would have conflicted with the ones our parents gave us.

We took on their beliefs in order to behave accordingly and to fit in whilst at school.

Then after school, as we went to college, university or to work, we started to pick up even more beliefs and viewpoints from different people and started to take things handed to us from the big wide world. Yes, we did what we could to now fit into that world.

All of this information, all the beliefs and all the opinions that are given to us from others, swims around in our mind. We take in yet more information from our experiences and we live life trying to figure this all out by using a combination of other people's rules and those of our own.

This is all confusing for our poor minds because all we are trying to do is be happy. It isn't too much to ask but we can easily get lost in all this noise.

As a kid you may have valued fun, comfort and adventure, and you had beliefs around how to get them values, like playing with your toys, having a cuddle with your mother and being read stories or using your imagination as you play in your home-made den.

Then as you grew you started to put other values ahead of these or at least in the mix, values like significance and gratitude. This then went some way to shaping your behaviour.

Whilst witnessing all of this, we come up with certain beliefs and attach meanings to things as we go. We believe different things at different stages of our lives.

When we're kids we believe that there is a monster under the bed that is going to grab our ankles each night. Then when we are adults we know that's not true...right?

We are jammed full of many beliefs for different parts of our lives and they all come together to help paint the picture and code our Matrix. Your beliefs are what you regard as the truths in life and how we label them things.

The different types of beliefs

There are obviously many different types of beliefs but I want to draw your attention to what we will talk about in this book, they are:

1. Macro beliefs and micro beliefs
2. Self-belief
3. Limiting beliefs
4. Modelling beliefs

Macro and Micro Beliefs

Your macro and micro beliefs are the personal convictions that you have about all kinds of things, you will have concluded these along the way and will have beliefs that make sense to you.

Macro beliefs are the global beliefs that we have, they are how we generalise things on a grand scale. You will hear a person's macro beliefs when they say sentences like *"Life is _ _ _", "I am _ _ _"* or *"People are _ _ _"*.

They are basically the blanket beliefs we have to generally sum things up.

Some macro beliefs of drivers are things like:

"Motorsport is only for the wealthy".
"I am rubbish at everything I do".
"All people in motorsport are sharks".

Can you imagine a driver with these three macro beliefs?

I don't think they would go very far because they would give up when they hit the first bump in the road.

Macro beliefs are the way we generalise things and these can be heavily responsible for our perspective in life, so we must make sure that these are accurate and paint the correct global picture for you.

Micro beliefs however are more specific, you can hear these when a person says a sentence that is structured with ***"If...then...".***

This is just like the specific belief that you have as you rule for meeting certain values.

In racing, some micro beliefs you will hear are:

"If another driver cuts me up then they are disrespecting me"
"If I learn sales skills then I can improve my chances of getting sponsorship"
"If I win this team over then they will help my career".

So your macro and micro beliefs are the beliefs that people most refer to, they form the way that you make sense of things.

Self-Belief

Your self-belief is the view you have of yourself. You can either be your biggest fan by focusing your attention on what good things you have to offer, or you can be your biggest critic and only focus on your shortcomings and dwell on them.

As a driver, self-belief is of huge importance. Without it you will go into races not believing that you can win, you will allow others to mentally bully you and you will not be able to keep your head above water as the challenges within motorsport flood in.

When a driver lacks self-belief and also has an overriding fear for what others think of them, then they will usually struggle when it comes to high pressure situations.

When in those times (like in an important race or when they are in the lead) they will let their mind think about the failure that they might experience if things don't go to plan and what people will say because of it.

Self-belief is basically a person's conviction that something can be done, and they are the person who can do it.

When you have self-belief in bucketful's then you will throw yourself into challenges just knowing that you will figure things out on the go. You basically trust yourself and do not worry too much about things not going to plan. You know that you will deal with whatever comes up.

Limiting Beliefs

As the name suggests, these beliefs are the beliefs that form your limitations.

When you have beliefs that allow you to strive and thrive in life then you give yourself permission to go full throttle, but when you have the kind of beliefs that limit your potential, then you are coasting through life with a governor fitted to your internal gas pedal.

Humans possess limiting beliefs to keep a lid on things. We use them to keep us safe and often to fit in with society. Some friends, loved ones and even some governments do not want you to believe in yourself too much because they either want to protect you from disappointment or to control you.

If you are mainly operating via your limiting beliefs then you can enjoy a life where you fit in and fly under the radar. Plus you can run less risk of experiencing the things that you don't like (your Avoidance Values).

But you know all too well that as a race driver you have chosen a path where limiting beliefs are not an option for you. You perform in an environment where you need to call upon your highest skills as a human in order to even compete in the first place. You need to allow your subconscious to operate freely with as few performance blockers as possible.

Limiting beliefs are some of the most stubborn little performance blockers that we have. They set the parameters of what is possible, they give us boundaries and cause us to walk a tightrope of what is acceptable.

Limiting beliefs are your enemy and must be dealt with.

This is what your Warrior Mind will battle with over time and will need to constantly monitor.

Your mind is the actual battlefield, so as a warrior you must be its commander. Limiting beliefs can be seen as an enemy so you must eliminate them or reform them.

You can have limiting beliefs around how far you can actually go, you can have limiting beliefs about the way the world works and you can have limiting beliefs about why you cannot get the results you want.

You can hear drivers express their limiting beliefs when they say things like:

"A driver can only do so much to make the car quick".
"The team is against me and might have given me the damaged chassis".
"I cannot succeed because I do not have the money".
"I cannot get sponsorship because I do not have the time".

These are the kind of limiting beliefs that cause you to lose hope and not give your all.

As a human you have a natural skill for being resourceful, you are good at figuring things out, but if you are being influenced by your limiting beliefs then you are no longer resourceful.

You may have self-belief but if you have put up walls around what can be done then you will still be limited.

Keeping your limiting beliefs at bay requires serious upkeep, you must constantly correct things when you start to limit yourself mentally, verbally or physically. If you don't then the walls will slowly be built around you and will gain momentum. Before you know it, you are boxed in.

Modelling beliefs

Something you may have heard of is modelling beliefs. This is a great brain hack that people use when they are trying to pick up a skill quickly.

In fact, a great portion of this book was designed from modelling others. The information and mental training has been modelled from people who have succeeded before you and from the personal development sciences that I have studied.

When modelling someone's belief system you are learning the very beliefs of that person who has achieved the results that you want. You are learning how they see the world and the beliefs that they operate with, you then copy those beliefs to see if they work for you. In other words you are doing what you can to copy their Matrix and how they mentally operate.

Let's get two more drivers to give an example. We will call these drivers Emma and James. Emma is super confident when it comes to fast corners, yet James struggles with them.

Beliefs of Emma

To understand why they differ so much, I would simply ask Emma to explain to me what she believes, what she thinks about and how she views high speed corners.

To start with she will probably tell me something stupidly simply like "I just keep it pinned".

Which is ok, because that tells us that she simplifies what a high speed corner means to her, she chunks the information together, thus she feels confident when driving them and just gets it done.

You will notice that when somebody is good at something, they simplify the actions they take when doing it.

Whereas someone who struggles with a particular part of their driving will over complicate the process and think too much about it. They make it sound more difficult than it actually is.

But if I was to ask her to go a bit deeper and get her to tell me more, like where she is looking as she enters the corner, what she is thinking, what simple rules she has about driving these types of corners and basically get her to describe her thought process, it wouldn't be long until she started to share the inner beliefs and viewpoints she has about high speed corners.

She may say things like:

"It's my job to keep the speed in the car and be smooth on all the inputs so I can use the aero".

"High speed corners are a great place to make time because most drivers cannot get themselves to take them quick, so I must".

"When approaching the corner I look into the apex super early".

"As I turn in all I think about and look for is the exit, so my vision is always far ahead".

"I get a buzz each time I am quickest in the high speed stuff, I make it a priority to get those corners sorted early on".

"When driving these corners I am direct with the steering but I am relaxed"

She may finish off by saying something like "I love fast corners".

By listening to a driver like this, you can get a feel for their beliefs, you learn a little about their technique and how they feel when driving those types of corners.

If you were to then take on some of her beliefs and outlook, then you would be 'Modelling' her belief system and by adopting what she does mentally you would improve the way you drive high speed corners.

Beliefs of James

Then if you were to ask James (who is way under par in the area of high speed corners) what his beliefs are for how to drive these types of corners then he may share things like this:

"High speed corners are difficult"

"The goal is to go as fast as I can without risking a crash".

"The car feels nervous so I am not too confident in these corners".

"When I approach the corner I just go as deep as I dare until I feel something in my chest telling me to lift".

"I sometimes think about the outside wall and how close it is, so if I make a mistake then I will have an almighty shunt".

"When going through these corners I grip the wheel as hard as I can and just hold on".

He might end with saying something like "I don't like high speed corners and I know that I need to improve there".

When you listen to drivers explaining things like this, it is easy to understand why the same corner can have very different reactions from them due to their beliefs of how to drive such a corner. They get different feelings and different results due to the way they view that type of corner and by the meaning they give it.

This all stems from their beliefs. If you were to model the beliefs and approach of James then you would hit the same problems as he does.

If you are driving and thinking about crashing or how close the walls are, then you are riddled with limiting beliefs that cause you to tighten up, this is never good for a driver.

The beauty of Modelling

So if you want to get a shortcut to learning a new skill or to improve something about your driving then the best thing to do is find someone who is getting the results that you want, and get into their mind.

Understand these things:

1. What they believe about that situation
2. What they focus on when in that situation
3. Even what they are doing with their physiology (muscle tension, inputs, breathing, facial expression, etc)

This mental copying technique is seen a lot in sports, Archery is big on this. Each movement of your body, your breathing, your beliefs and what you are focusing on are all game changers as you look down that arrow. This is the same for every discipline or skill.

Copying the Matrix of someone who is excellent at doing something is one of the best mind hacks that we have got.

Once you know these things then you can either add some of them to what you are doing or completely copy them to see how it works for you.

I suggest when you do this that you go all in. Pretend that you are them to start with and see things through the eyes of the person you are modelling.

This works for driving as much as anything else. Even if as a driver you want to get better at public speaking, at selling, even at asking people out for a date, then learn from the best and model how they operate and what they do.

This is pretty much what a coach does, they go out and do what they can to model success, they try it out for themselves to prove it works, then they teach it to people. But you can coach yourself by following this process.

Obviously you need to go out and do it for real but if you copy the main beliefs and Matrix of someone then you can speed up the learning process and shorten the time it takes to reach your goals. People have successfully walked your path already so you may as well learn from them.

As I just briefly mentioned, if you wanted to thoroughly model someone's behaviour then on top of their beliefs you would also copy what they focus on and their physiology. So if a driver who is good at high speed corners lifts their vision up into the corner more, if they put their focus down the road more, if they relax their body and breath slowly, then copy these as well.

We will talk about this in the emotions chapter but to create the mental state you want you need to combine both your mind and body. When modelling someone, in copying the beliefs, focus and physiology, you are automatically creating the same emotions within yourself that they are.

That's what I want you to do to speed up your progress.

Take on the beliefs and rules of warriors, of the genuine champions out there and you will advance quicker.

Other terms that relate to your beliefs

Time and time again you will hear me refer to the words **meaning** and **translation.**

They are pretty much the same things but because they are related to your beliefs I want to be clear on what I mean by these two words.

When you hear me say 'meaning', I am referring to the meaning that you give things. These are the beliefs you have about things in the world.

A very popular saying is:

Change the meaning, change the feeling.

If you really take control of what things mean to you then you start to control your emotions.

People attach their own meaning to things. For instance if someone was to lose their drive, then they could have a few reactions to that based on their values and the meaning that they give this incident.

Some drivers will be devastated and will give it a meaning like "That's it, I am finished. Once a driver is dropped it is over for them".

Whereas other drivers will **translate** the situation differently by giving it a different **meaning**, they may react to it by saying "Ok what's done is done, the team is entitled to their opinion. I am thankful for the platform and career boost they gave me up to now because that will make it easier for me to get another drive".

Which one of these drivers is correct?

They are both correct.

They are both right because that's the way they believe it is and this will determine their actions that will prove their viewpoint. One will give up whilst the other will use what they have done up to now to create further opportunities.

Each time I say **meaning** I am referring to the meaning that you give things, and when I say **translation**, then this is the way you translate a certain incident in your mind. So they are very closely linked but slightly different.

You can either go through life translating things to help you or you can let them hinder you. What you believe about situations can be your secret weapon for handling stress and becoming a leader.

You are the one who gets to decide whether a tough time that you are going through is either the end or the beginning. It will either make you or break you. You get to decide that.

My question to you is this... Are you going to translate the world on your terms or are you going to do what most people do and allow the world to defeat them and decide for them?

These are questions that I will only ask people who want to possess the Warrior's Mind.

I think you know which perspective will help you most. As long as you are not being too delusional about things and as long as you remain self aware of your true situation then seeing things in a way that helps you move forward is always the way to go in my opinion.

It's up to you to label things in a way that helps you advance. This is being resourceful and part of being a warrior.

Situations will present themselves and it is up to you to see how they can be used, not how they are going to finish you.

Summary

Beliefs are a big deal when it comes to you enhancing your mental performance so when you are rebuilding your Matrix, they are one of the first ports of call to attend to.

First we see what your values are to understand what your mind is focused on and how to reach fulfilment, then we understand the best rules to have in place to meet those values, then we get down to the specific beliefs that support all of this.

You will be forever modifying your values, rules and beliefs during your life depending on what becomes important to you, so this will be a lifetime of refining.

In the training exercise that follows you will get to know some of your current beliefs, you will choose which ones have and haven't been serving you and you will start to build a new set of beliefs that will help you become the warrior you need to become.

Training Exercise – Your Beliefs

For this exercise you will see what beliefs you have been operating from and decide whether they need adjusting and if you think it's time for a belief system upgrade.

Our beliefs contribute to our perception of life and cause us to react a certain way. Change your beliefs and you literally change a major part of your internal coding.

To make it easy I have split this into steps and once you understand what to do, open up your WM Workbook and you can fill it out in the relevant spaces.

Here we will target the beliefs that have been holding you back, then after that we will move forward by committing to a new way of seeing things and to pick some people that you can learn from.

Here are the steps:

Step 1: Expose your limiting beliefs

First things first, let's expose the certain beliefs that are not helping you. The beliefs that form your excuses for why you cannot achieve the results you want and the limiting beliefs that you also have about yourself.

These may be things like:

"I can't drive quickly because I am not a natural driver".
"I don't have the time to do what I need to do".
"I don't have the money so there is no point in trying".
"I don't have the connections so will never make it".
"I never win at anything, so what's the point?".

Yes, limiting beliefs can also come in the form of a question. If you ask a crappy question then you will get a crappy answer that will cause you to feel crappy, perform crappy and get crappy results.

So be very careful of the questions you ask yourself. If you improve the quality of your questions you will get better answers and react in a different way.

What are some of the beliefs that bring you down and either create an upfront excuse for not giving this your all, or prevent you from going full out?

What are the beliefs that you know are not true but you are still hiding behind anyway?

If someone was to ask you, why haven't you succeeded as a driver yet, what would be some of your answers?

You may just find out your limiting beliefs by the excuses that come out of your mouth when answering questions like this.

I want you to think of at least two limiting beliefs and write them down in your Warrior's Mind Workbook.

Then we will carry on.

Step 2: What will happen?

This is where we play with your destiny line or at least ask yourself, what will my racing really look like in a year's time if I operate my mind with these beliefs and with this outlook?

Write it down.

Go for the worst case scenario to get it to move you even more. Make this as painful as you can, picture it.

Once you feel it and you get the mind thinking, "I must change the way I am seeing things here", then move on to step 3.

Step 3: Flip them

If you were to take these few limiting beliefs that are not helping you, that are crippling your progress, and you were to flip them, what would these beliefs be then?

So if before you had a belief that started with *"I don't have the time to ___"*, and you know full well that this belief is not serving you in the slightest, and you want to change it, then you could change it to something like *"I have got the same time as everyone else. I will make the time!"*.

In living by this new flipped belief you will have the feeling that this would be a person who doesn't want to experience the Avoidance Value of regret, and wants to give this everything they have.

They would rather fail in their pursuit for what they love, instead of only giving 50% and living the rest of their life regretting their half-assed attempt.

How can you flip your beliefs, reverse them, so they serve you and create a different outlook?

Again play with this, you don't need to get it spot on first time, we can change and rechange our beliefs as many times as we want.

Go for it.

Step 4: What happens then?

If you were to run with these new, flipped beliefs, then how good could things turn out then in twelve months time?

Visualize it and see what you could create if you were a person who had these two empowering beliefs driving them.

At the very least, succeed or fail, they would have a blast trying.

Step 5: Decide, commit and prove it

To live with these empowering beliefs that will help you reach a higher level is totally within your control to do so. You just need to decide to run with them.

This is all done consciously and with effort to start with.

As soon as you old limiting beliefs come in, you need to quickly break that thought process and slam your new empowering belief in place as quickly as you can.

Your new empowering beliefs can be seen as your weapon of choice in this instance. You beat down your old beliefs until they submit and until your mind let's them go and you keep your new beliefs big in your mind. Use them to dictate how you show up each day.

Step 6: Three people to model

Once you have done the first five steps, you can then pick out some people who you wish to learn from. You can pick drivers that you admire or people outside of our sport.

Fill your head full of their quotes, their autobiographies, watch their interviews and if they are still alive then see if you can go talk with them.

These people have succeeded before you so when you spend time with them, either virtually or in person, you pick up their beliefs and you start to subconsciously apply them.

Write at least three names down and start searching for ways you can consume their thought process.

That's it!

Thanks for taking the time to do this, once your old beliefs have been exposed and you have committed to changing them, and you have named some mentors, we can carry on to the next chapter.

Building Material No.4 – Your Knowledge

CHAPTER FIFTEEN

Building Material No. 4 – Your Knowledge

"Knowledge is power"

Francis Bacon

It would be a mistake to overlook the importance of your knowledge when it comes to creating your Matrix.

I am not sure if you have seen Elon Musk's third interview with Joe Rogan which was published on Spotify on 11th February 2021, but if you listen to Elon then you will be astonished at just how much he knows about his craft.

Whether he is talking about space travel, the universe, car manufacturing, atoms, protons, technology, smart phones and any other subject related to his companies, you can just tell that he is super hands on and makes sure that he knows as much as he possibly can.

A lot of drivers may know how to turn in a good lap time but they are often not so switched on when it comes to their sport and all that is associated with it.

They just want to turn up and drive, they do not take the time to fully master their craft or learn engineering, sponsorship and everything else that they need to get down in order to succeed.

Real champions are smart

It is a common belief that race drivers do not have a brain and are not the sharpest tool in the box, but all of the super quick and true champion drivers that I have personally worked with or competed against have all impressed me by their intelligence.

Ok they may not be fully up to speed with general knowledge and mathematics, but when it comes to industry specific things they are very switched on.

They go deep into car setup; they learn all they can about the engine and how it wants to be driven. They work on understanding and feeling how the car wants to be driven. They read a race amazingly well whilst in the car and know exactly what they want changing on the car setup wise.

Become a master of your craft

This puts the emphasis on you to ensure that you have the racing intelligence that you need and that you study all parts of your sport to make sure that you are not just a 'dumb driver' who just knows how to drive in circles.

We have spoken a lot about mental coding, but when it comes to your knowledge we can say that this also falls underneath the area of mental data. It contributes to your Matrix.

There is motorsport specific knowledge that will help your mind make the best decisions and see things correctly. You must keep feeding your mind the correct intelligence it needs so it can make the right decisions and operate using accurate information.

You must master your craft, that includes you being clued up in the following areas:

- The actual driving and how your car needs to be driven
- Car setup
- Having the feel for what the car is doing in the corners
- Being able to communicate this to the engineer
- Understanding engineering a little
- Circuit knowledge
- A good level of understanding about physical training and your own body
- Know about opportunities in the driver market (drives available)
- People and leadership skills
- The business of motorsport
- Sponsorship
- Sales and marketing

If you approach your sport correctly and put in the dedication that it takes to become a real champion, then this is more than a full-time job. You must study your craft and become an expert on your industry.

This even comes down to knowing the names of the people in your team and understanding what makes them tick.

You must be more switched than the majority of drivers and take your destiny into your own hands.

You must become an expert in your field.

When a warrior goes to battle they make sure that they master their sword (or whatever weapon they have), they analyse and study their enemy, they learn the various fighting styles, they are students of war, they take the time to understand the patterns of a battle and make it their responsibility to become as knowledgeable as they can in all areas.

In doing this they have armed their minds with the knowledge that will not only give them the edge over their enemy but it also helps them feed their minds with facts that will help them win and not misinformation that will mislead them.

Their mission and their life depend on that knowledge.

How is this any different to you?

When you get to the higher levels, especially in endurance racing, you quickly learn the importance of being smart. Pretty much all of the top drivers are switched on and if you haven't taken the time to study your sport and know your stuff, then you quickly get exposed and the team look to your teammate for the answers they need.

Don't let that happen.

Train yourself

The knowledge part of your mastery is down to you to manage, to plan and to follow through on.

Training Exercise – Your Knowledge

This training exercise is very straight forward.

Simply write down the certain things that you must learn about and master in order to be a better driver and help your mind use facts so your Matrix is as full with accurate data.

I have split things up into certain areas within your WM Workbook so you can start to list what you need to study in there.

After you have done this please schedule in a couple of hours per week that you will dedicate to pure learning. It can be a different subject each week to keep things fresh.

If you can learn something of value for ten hours per month then you will be building yourself into a driver with a real racing brain.

Again, your simulator can be used as a fairly good tool for learning set up.

Building Material No.5 – Your Past

CHAPTER SIXTEEN

Building Material No.5 – Your Past

> **"**
> *"You do not move ahead by constantly looking in a rear*
> *view mirror"*
> *Warren W. Wiersbe*

It nearly goes without saying that our Matrix is also heavily influenced by what we have lived through in our past.

Many of our beliefs and automatic responses stemmed from what we have experienced earlier on in life. We learn from everything that we go through and take on that information to assist us going forward. Or we use it to hold us back.

Our past can help us in both positive and negative ways so with you being a person who needs to consistently perform at a higher level, then this is an area that you should pay attention to.

Your mind uses your past as proof for how things work in the world, as a kid you learned not to touch that hot stove or iron by once touching it. So the past has its uses as an education tool but all too often there are certain parts of our past that we may hang on to that are no longer serving us today.

When I'm working with someone on their mental performance, even though for 99% of the time we focus on now and on the future, we must always spend a little time looking into their past so we can understand where their behaviour may have come from, and what may have contributed to their current mental coding.

Two kinds

There are two kinds of 'pasts' that we will refer to in this book, there is the past in your normal life and there is the past in your racing life.

We are going to separate them because even though both affect you in the current time, I want us to become more specific on things.

Normal Life Past - These are the things that you have experienced in your life outside the car, kart, bike, plane or boat (whatever you are racing).

This could be what you went through at school, at college, at home, as you grew up and any other time before this very day.

We all have things from our past that need to be dealt with or learned from so when understanding things about yourself it is worth quickly shining a torch on it.

Racing Past - This refers to your past and the experiences that you have had in your racing world.

These could be moments and memories from previous times on track, in the paddock and any other area related to your racing life.

How our past can affect us now

Your past is a big subject and talking about it thoroughly would take another book, so to over-simplify it for the purpose of this book and to cut straight to the chase, I have split it into two more areas.

The two ways are:

1) How your past can give you auto responses to things.
2) How your past can give you a story that you use now.

Let me explain.

Your past creates Auto Responses

Firstly our past creates seemingly automatic responses to things.

In *normal life* (as a kid) there could have been a time when you were tormented by your siblings one day when they threw a big hairy spider into your sleeping bag. This single incident could then be the catalyst for you having a slight or major spider phobia in the present day.

In your *racing life,* you may have once been talked into taking a high speed corner without lifting the throttle (flat out). When you tried it you ended up having an almighty crash that ended up hurting you a little and cost you a fortune to repair the car. The auto response you get now is that you often seem to lift out of risky situations on track or in high speed corners. Plus you no longer trust what people tell you.

Your mind learns through experience, so some past experiences can help you whilst other past experiences can still be acting as a performance blocker right now.

If a certain episode in life is painful or alarming enough, even if it only happened once, it's amazing how the brain will totally ignore all the other times you slept in a sleeping bag with no spider or how many other times you took a corner flat out with no harm, and it will focus on that one time that it didn't go well.

You notice this about your parents or other people when they keep giving you a hard time about being late or making another mistake, even though you were only late once or made a certain mistake once, the other hundred times you did what you were supposed to.

Annoying huh?

Well that is the same kind of thing for how your mind remembers your past.

That's the power of Pain. It leaves a bigger mark in your mind and in your memory.

Our past creates certain beliefs, and these are going to influence our beliefs system, our decisions and our overall Matrix.

Your past gives you a story

The second thing that our past gives us is a story that we either hide behind or constantly tell ourselves in the current day.

We have all done this from time to time where we use a past event as a story for why we will not let our guard down or we will tell others about it to get some kind of connection, reaction or some sympathy from them.

We use it as our reason for why we are currently acting a certain way or why we have certain viewpoints.

In *normal life*, you could have been left devastated when your childhood sweetheart cheated on you or when you had something else happen that made you the victim.

In your *racing life*, you may have been suckered in by a dishonest manager, got screwed over in a driver shootout, had someone in the team stab you in the back or you may have been dropped from a driver program.

This is something that wasn't entirely your fault but things that were done to you where you got the short end of the stick.

I think most of us have had times when we have had something bad happen to us and life has dished us some seriously bad luck. That's life as they say.

But again these things can shape us.

When we have something unjust happen to us we often hang on to that past memory and use it as our story in life. We tell people that we are acting a certain way because this happened to us in the past.

Even though our past has now gone we can still allow it to take up our mind in the present day and let it influence us now. This can be a good thing because we use it as a lesson, but often we also use bad experiences as an ongoing excuse for why we are not fully showing up today.

You can hear someone using their past as a self-limiting story when they say things like *"I don't trust people in relationships, I was once screwed over, if I get into a relationship it will only happen again"* or *"I don't deserve success, life has it in for me. Did I tell you about that time I got dropped from the driver program?"*

When we use our past as something to hide behind or to create self-limiting beliefs from then it builds a Matrix that will cause us pain in the long run. Even if we succeed in our career, we will still remain unfulfilled in life.

We do things for a positive intent

There is a common belief in psychology that every action we take is done with some kind positive intent in mind.

Whether we are harming or helping others, treating yourself well or physically self-harming, taking action or procrastinating, we take those actions to meet some internal need or to escape some kind of pain.

Due to our minds using pain as a tool for education and due to our human desire to be 'loved' by others, it is of no surprise that we let our past into the present moment.

Subconsciously reliving our past, experiencing the feelings that it gives us even though it was a long time ago, and using our past as a story is all done for some positive intent.

It's not until we deal with that past by associating pain to holding on to it, or by becoming aware of how much it is holding us back, do we actually do something about it.

So in short, I am saying that if you are to have a free mind, a mind that allows you to create a Warrior Mind that will serve you best, then you must use your past to support you rather than bring you down.

If you want to do this thoroughly and are seriously struggling with how your past is sabotaging your life now, then I suggest you see a professional who can help you address it. I will offer you techniques for overcoming your past within this chapter, but without personal 1:1 interaction with a trained specialist, you may do the exercises incorrectly or not thoroughly enough.

It is worth doing this correctly, we must put your first here.

Dealing with your past

In saying that, if you are determined to overcome your past by yourself and only have mild interference from your past, then I will share some of the techniques that worked very well for me and my clients.

A great part of the magic for doing this depends on the way you translate it.

Core beliefs that help you

Remembering that our beliefs are largely responsible for the way we see things, if you want to change the way you feel about your past then having some fundamental core beliefs about it can really start the ball rolling for you.

One of the main beliefs that personally helped change my life, when it came to my past, was this...

Everything happens for a reason and a purpose and it serves you.

These twelve words really are some of the most potent twelve words that you can live by and once you fully believe them, and prove how true they are, then you can fully move forward.

If you believe that everything that has happened can benefit you in some way, no matter how twisted it could be, and it may just be life's way of teaching you something, then suddenly you start to translate your past in a different way.

You start to see the message that it is trying to give you.

Here are some things that happen to us all and ways of using these experiences to help you.

If it was something that was done to you, when someone came into your life and harmed you in some way, then this was a lesson in life that should make you sharper and help you notice people or situations like this in the future. The incident may have been your tipping point and caused you then to get rid of them out of your life before they did even more damage. If you exposed them for it then you may have prevented others from falling for the same trap.

If you made a stupid mistake, then welcome to life, as humans we make some of the most stupid and embarrassing mistakes (and lots of them). You would have been in a certain state of mind where it made sense in the moment to do what you did but afterwards you realised that it was completely stupid. That is totally normal.

Remember what the word is, mistake, or Miss Take. We are all about mastering translation and seeing things in a way that helps us. Well, seeing the word mistake as the term Miss Take, gives you the understanding that you get to go again. You may have missed last time, but you get another take, another go.

If you should have made a different decision. We go through life making decisions every second of the day, you cannot continue to punish yourself years after the incident for making a few of those decisions incorrectly or for temporarily acting out of character. That is mental-self-harm.

You need to stand by your decisions because there would have been a reason for making them at the time and it would have made sense on some level back then.

I have heard drivers say things like "Ah, I shouldn't have gone for that move in the race" after they climbed their way up from the back of the grid but then ended up crashing with another car near the end of the race.

I will always react the same way to these kind of regrets by saying "Are you kidding me?!? You only got into that position because of your bold moves. Yes it didn't work out in the end but boy you put on a show".

When you are attacking in a race and you know that you need to make many overtakes to regain a good position, then obviously you run the risk of one of them moves not coming off. You have to take that approach otherwise you will remain at the back.

I also hear people beating themselves up for making the wrong life decisions, where they should have gone for that job or put the money on that other horse.

But what people always forget is the rule of '**everything happens for a reason and a purpose**'.

Ok if you had taken the other job or put money on that other horse then in theory you would be in a better position, but life isn't that simple, because in making a different decision you have gone down a different life path.

Watch the film called The Butterfly Effect to understand how this can mess things up.

You could have been run over on the road and killed one day as you were going to that new job or when on the way to the betting shop to pick up your winnings. Each decision takes you down a different path and you never know what the repercussions will be.

So you should never beat yourself up over decisions because you never know what would have happened as a consequence, good or bad.

How your past can harm your current life

When it comes to your past you need to remind yourself that what happened, happened, it has gone. Hence why we call it the past.

Our past is no longer here or it is not even relevant to what is going on in our lives today. However, we often keep the past with us due to us allowing ourselves to replay the event over and over again into the current time.

Dragging your old life's baggage into your new life only ends up in disaster or causes the past to happen all over again. This is the same for drivers in their cars as it is for people in their relationships.

If you go into a new relationship being cautious and by having your 'walls up' because you have been hurt in the past, then you will most likely sabotage that new relationship and it will fall apart. When this happens your mind will see what's going on and will say things like "See, it's happening again, I told you all men are pigs!".

When in fact you may have just ruined what could have been your dream relationship just because you didn't allow yourself to open up and show the real you. You may have acted jealous at times or you may not have trusted them even though they did nothing wrong, and this was all because you were scared of being hurt again.

This then supports an inaccurate beliefs system that you have about relationships and before you know it history keeps repeating itself. It's a vicious never ending mental cycle but it happens a lot.

That is a prime example of the trap that living in our past creates for us.

What links all your past moments?

The one overriding truth that I want you to always remember is that everything that happens in our past can be learned from and can positively serve you or others if you want it to.

If someone hurt you, then you can help others overcome it when they go through the same.

If you hurt someone and it still bothers you now, then you know that you did something against your morals, and certainly won't do it ever again.

If you did something 'stupid', then that's just something we have all done at some point. That memory can help you judge others less for their occasional 'stupid' actions and realise that nobody is perfect.

I mean nobody. Even the people we admire have got up to some crazy stuff.

If you made the 'wrong' decision, then you know that you have power to direct your life. That may have been one wrong turn that you made back then, but this means that you can make a couple more decisions in the right direction and you will be back on track.

Having the ability to make decisions in the first place means that you are powerful. You have control over your destiny. A wrong turn is a reminder of that. Feel empowered by these decisions.

Again, everything you have gone through helps you grow or helps you teach others to help them grow.

All these experiences have helped create a wiser you and a more educated individual. They have shown that you can survive them, so you are stronger than you think.

What else do you need to explain exactly what a warrior is?

A warrior is a person who has been through battles, who has the scars to prove it, they've made bad decisions that could have even cost the lives of others, but in doing so they eventually become the wise warrior that can then press on and have the knowledge needed to do it better next time and reach their North Star.

You are that warrior, but if you let your past cripple you instead of using it to build you up, then you will forever be a slave to time gone by.

The decision is really yours for how you handle your past life.

Change your past

Talking of decisions, there is something else you can decide about the past events that may be holding you back. You can decide to change the way you see them.

Two effective ways to handle your past memories:

1. Change the way you replay them in your head.
2. Change the way you are translating them now.

Change the way you replay them

Our past experiences are only still with us because we replay them in our mind in some way or we will have certain triggers in life now that remind us of our past and in doing so it brings it all up again.

There are many mental techniques and procedures taught through Hypnotherapy, Neuro Linguistic Programming (NLP), Cognitive Behavioural Therapy (CBT) and the many other therapies that we have at our disposal now, and they all work.

Most of them teach you how to see things in a different way and quieten down the noise you get from the past events that are affecting you. Some therapies will consciously talk you through the process whilst others will be closed eye exercises where you play with the size, shape, colour, sound, volume and the overall way in which you see the memory in your head.

Most of them will give you a sense of the inner strength so you feel powerful and maybe dissociate yourself with the past event.

If you have something you are struggling to get past, then I suggest that you do some research and see if learning techniques or going to experts in these therapies could be something for you.

Something we have a lot of in the world now are psychologists and therapists, so never feel like you are on your own.

We are all here to help you.

Change the way you translate them

For me this is the big one. It is again using your translation skills so you can consciously associate different things to your past, and in turn feel differently about it.

You do this by answering one simple question:

Can I change or rectify what happened?

If the answer is yes, then do it.

If the answer is no, and you cannot change what is done, then simply answer this next question - **How can I use it to help me progress in a positive and empowering way?**

In simple terms we are just using that past event that hurt or made us angry so much, in a way that serves us today.

If we can't change the event, then we may as well change how it makes us feel now.

One of my dislikes in life is living with regret, that is one of my main Avoidance Values.

As soon as I began using my unfortunate past memories as moments that would actually help me grow (personal growth being a Target Value of mine), then my mind quickly associated gratitude to those past events.

I believe that I would not be a particularly good coach if I had done things perfectly in life and was gifted an easy life. I need my screw ups to help me coach others.

That is how the things from your past can help you help others. It is all data that you can use to advance yourself and those around you. In seeing things this way you become more grateful for the 'bad things' that you have experienced.

You are coaching you

You may be focused on your racing right now but you are the one person who is in your head, you can either be your biggest fan or your biggest critic.

You are constantly self-coaching and talking yourself through life. You need to also experience unfortunate moments in your past in order to coach yourself better right now.

Your past is a blessing.

You won the life lottery to be here in the first place, and to even have a past is a pure privilege.

Once you start to realise that you are on a journey and whilst on this journey that everything that happens contributes to your life experience and all helps you in some way, no matter how twisted that may seem or how it is presented to you, your past events are all gifts.

This is not positive mental attitude; this again is seeing things in a way that serves you best.

Then it becomes the truth.

You can see how these kinds of viewpoints can help you build a powerful outlook on life (Matrix).

You decide

It is totally up to you how you deal with your past, but I strongly recommend that you jump on this if you feel that it is an area that may be hampering you.

A warrior needs to march on so if you want to get to your desired destination then you must strip away the past memories that are weighing you down. That baggage is making your journey so much harder.

Are you going to use your past to help make you stronger, or are you going to allow it to turn you into a victim? You decide.

Training Exercise – Your Past

There are numerous ways to help you overcome your past but for this training exercise I want to use one of my personal favourites.

If you have a past or something that happened that keeps causing you to hesitate or prevent you from being at your best, then this can work nicely if done correctly.

We will use a mixture of visualization and conscious mental work when doing this.

Visualization exercise

When it comes to your past, we can again use your timeline and do two things. Firstly, you can use the destiny line to see what happens to your life if you carry on holding onto your past and let it destroy your future.

As you can tell, I really like using pain to help us change our ways.

Secondly you can go back in time, using your timeline again if you prefer, and revisit your past experiences that still mentally bully you now.

The great thing about visualization is that you can play with the past and the future, plus you can modify past events so they look differently and as a result you feel differently about them.

You will be surprised at just how effective mental representation of your past events is. If you ask people who have overcome tough pasts and no longer let it affect them, they will tell you that they just don't really picture those things anymore. The memories are at the back of their mind now and have no power over them anymore.

You can use that same approach yourself. If you change the pictures in your mind about your past events then the feelings also change.

If you go back to something that happened in the past and you pull that memory slide out and take a look at it then you may see it as a clear memory.

When we have memories that we constantly go back to and often replay in our mind, we see them as big, bold, colourful pictures that have a lot of detail. When we think of these memories it may even be in first person so it's as if it is all happening again, and we feel it.

Well as a visualization exercise, you can play with the qualities (submodalities) of that picture or movie that we have in our head and in doing so we can reduce the impact it has on us.

This sounds a bit far-fetched but when you get good at this you can literally change the way you feel about things just by changing the internal representation that you have of these moments.

When people say "I have put that memory at the back of my mind", it reminds me of this exercise because if we have something that we remember a lot, then it is often at the front of our mind and we can recall it all. Well, we are using that very principle to change things.

So if you go back on your timeline to when you had a certain past experience that you want to feel less emotion towards, then you can pull that memory up and play with it.

You can:

- Shrink that sucker down.
- Turn it black and white.
- Push it far away into the distance so you cannot really see what's going on anymore.
- Make it fuzzy and out of focus.

You can even pick it up and crush it up as you would if you were crushing an empty eggshell in your fist.

You can represent it in your mind however you want, even create a burning furnace and throw it in.

Whatever it takes for you to change the way your mind sees it.

Each time you think about it, you do this and train that dog of a mind a new trick. That trick is how to destroy the feelings that this memory gives you.

Talking of dogs you can even visualize that your memory is being posted through an imaginary letterbox and each time it is posted, a dog being a dog, comes along and tears it up into pieces.

This is something to play with and even have fun with. You can spring clean your past using your imagination and your visualized timeline and even have the people within the memory dressed up like Bugs Bunny.

The voices that haunt from within certain memories can be changed to sound like Mickey Mouse's voice so you can actually start to laugh at the memory. This is a clever way to change your association with them and your automated responses.

To back this all up and to counteract 'bad' memories that you don't like, you can dust off some of the good memories that you had from the past. The ones that you haven't mentally revisited for some time now, the ones that may fill you full of gratitude as you think back to them.

These are the memories that should be big, bold, colourful and at the forefront of your mind.

Always remember - You feel what you focus on.

Choose to change or translate

I want to repeat this from earlier because it is important that you do this as a training exercise.

To do this on a more conscious level, you can change the way you think about your past events by asking yourself some questions.

The first question is - **Can I change that past event?**

You are asking whether you can do anything about what happened back then. Is it possible to rectify or change the situation at all?

If so, then do what you can to do that.

If not, or if you tried but it isn't possible, then it's time to ask the second question - **How can I translate that past event so it serves me in some way?**

How can you see it in a way that helps you move on and progress in life?

Is there a twisted lesson from it all?

Will it allow you to help and advise others who go through the same situation?

Does it make you wiser to those types of people or situations?

Has it given you skills or knowledge that you wouldn't otherwise have had?

Has it led to you meeting someone special in your life now, someone you may not have had the chance to meet otherwise?

If we can't change what happened, then we certainly can change the way we translate it in our mind, the way we see it (the meaning we attach to it).

This is totally your call and because it was you that went through it, you have earned the right to see it how you want.

You get to say what your past means, you get to choose how you feel about it and you get to decide how it will affect you from now on.

You are now in control.

Building Material No.6 – Your Influences

CHAPTER SEVENTEEN

Building Material No.6 – Your Influences

> ❝
>
> *"Stand guard at the door of your mind"*
> *Jim Rohn*

The final area of your Matrix that I want to talk about are your influences.

When I say your influences I am referring to the certain things you have in your daily life that are influencing your thoughts and your mindset.

The things that we have spoken about already (your values, rules, beliefs, knowledge and past) all influence you but now I am talking about everything else both internally and externally.

The main things that influence us are:

- People (family members, friends, loved ones, other drivers, team members)
- What you listen to (music, audiobooks, podcasts)
- What you watch (movies, shows, in the external world)

- Your environment (your surroundings and living standards)
- Your internal focus (self talk, pictures in your mind)

Our minds are very easily manipulated and directed by our surroundings and the people within it. When approaching this topic I want you to remember this chapter's quote from Jim Rohn:

"Stand guard at the door of your mind"

Jim Rohn was one of the pioneers in modern personal development and when he preached this quote he was stating the importance of you consciously governing what you allow into your mind.

In his own way he would remind people that the world has many influencers within it, some that are good for us and some that are toxic for us, so if you want to help your mind perform as you want then you had better fill it with information that helps it do that.

I am totally on board with Jim Rohn here, the people we hang with, what we listen to, what we watch and the environment that we live in all come together and cause us to act and think in a certain way. So you'd better make sure that the information you are taking in, whether directly or indirectly, supports you and allows you to maintain the Matrix that you need.

Derren Brown

If you are aware of Derren Brown then you may have seen some of his mental experiments and how good he is at influencing people.

There was one show of his that sticks in my mind, it was called Toy Story and in it he demonstrated the power of Perception Without Awareness (PWA).

PWA is when we take in information that guides our thoughts and decision making without us being consciously aware of it. People refer to this kind of mind influencing as subliminal, but researchers nowadays have decided that subliminal is actually invisible stimuli that can influence us. Whereas PWA is a little more obvious and can come in many different forms.

For this show Derren met with a lady called Alice in a large toy store and he was letting her pick a toy from the store. She could choose any toy from the 250,000 toys that were stocked there.

After quickly walking her around the store he then asked her to go off on her own and choose whatever toy she wanted.

She was instructed to not physically pick up the toy, just mentally decide which one she wants, without showing any body language giveaways towards her chosen toy. She went off into the store on her own with nobody watching.

Once done, she then went back to Derren and following a bit of showmanship, he then proceeded to single out the very toy that she had mentally picked out.

Spoil alert here...but it was a cuddly giraffe toy.

How did he know this?

Well, he influenced her to choose that toy by using giraffe specific visual and audible cues. As he was initially showing her around the store and talking to her, he would drop in giraffe references. There was one point when he asked Alice **"Giraffe a favourite toy when you were little?"**.

The way he pronounced it sounded like he said **"Did you have a favourite toy when you were little?"**.

Consciously she didn't notice that he said giraffe but Derren was hoping that she picked it up subconsciously. Very clever.

Then dotted around the toy story were many giraffe 'subliminals' like giraffe T-Shirts, giraffe patterns on the wall and letters spelling the word giraffe hanging from the ceiling.

When you re-watch the show you can see many more clever ways in which Derren was implanting the thought of giraffe into her mind without her realising. They were everywhere but you only notice once you know what the plan is.

Then when it came to her choosing a toy she naturally decided to go for the giraffe.

She believed that it was her free will that chose that toy, when it was actually a thought that was put there for her.

How we experience this

This is again a reminder of how much we are on autopilot and how we are partially directed by the things around us.

I know that the Derren Brown experiment was just a show and the sceptics among us will say that it was a set up but you must admit that you will have experienced many similar times when something on a smaller scale has happened to you.

Maybe when someone mentioned a certain food and then all of a sudden all you could think about was that food.

Your parents would have been masters at this, there would have been times when they influenced your behaviour using PWA. There may have been times when they wanted you to figure something out without them directly telling you, they may have done this to avoid an argument with you or they may have wanted you to use your common sense with something and seem like you made your own decision.

Either way they would have done a Derren Brown on you at some point to influence you to take a certain action. Or a partner may do this when he or she wants to be taken out on a date, they may leave the restaurant advert up on their phone or suggest that they are hungry and it has been such a long time since you have gone out together. Then all of a sudden you come up with the great idea to take them out for dinner. You genius you.

People

As you will recall, one of our greatest values and needs in life is to feel loved and to be significant, it's just how we are. So with this in mind we are most influenced by the people we have in our lives.

Their views, their behaviour and their actions all influence us, and to fit in and meet our values we often copy those views, behaviours and actions. This could be our friends, our family members, loved ones, people in racing or even the people we admire in life that we have never even met in person.

The big one for drivers is the people they hang out with. If you are a driver who always hangs with other drivers that get drunk each weekend when not racing, then you will soon join them and be a part of that group.

As you can imagine, this soon turns into you getting the reputation in the industry and, well, let's just say that things happen that could get you into trouble.

I am not saying that you shouldn't go out for drinks here by the way, I am just showing you how influential our friends can be.

This 'need' for fitting in causes us to be easily influenced and you will notice as you go through life that you may befriend different types of people (who like different things) depending on what stage you are personally going through. When you are aged eight to eleven years old most of your friends may have been top of the class and because you were close with them you may have also improved your own grades.

But then when you got to twelve years old you noticed that these friends weren't cool enough for you and you started to hang around with the kids who were getting into trouble and going against the system. Then all of a sudden your viewpoints, beliefs and behaviour changes and before you know it you are in the headmaster's office for yet another telling off.

Then when you leave school you may get bored of these friends and move on to the next group and again your viewpoint and even your goals change.

Another well used quote is:

If you hang with 9 broke friends, then you'll be the 10th

As harsh as it sounds, your friends are super important for your mindset and your career, so as a driver who wants to make it and as a person who wants to achieve a Warrior's Mind you need to make sure that you spend time with people who help you achieve these things.

If not then you may just be better off going alone for a while as you graft on your craft.

You just know when you are with people who you are not aligned with. I remember the very time that I realised I needed to change something. I wanted to be a race driver yet here I was in the back of a crowded car as we drove around after midnight up to no good. The rave music (yes I said rave, I am that old) was blasting from the aftermarket speakers, the car was full of people smoking and I was just sitting there thinking "This isn't me any more".

I felt out of place. As my goals become more important then so did my identity, the way I saw myself. Soon after that I decided to go full tilt towards becoming a race driver. In doing so I had to spend way less time with my current friends and virtually all my time went into working, preparing my car, building my racing profile and searching for sponsors.

It was awkward and uncomfortable at the time, and you have to put up with the sceptical minds of your friends, but I have to say that it played out well for me. Who knows where I would have ended up otherwise.

Same for you. You may not be in that kind of situation but just know that people are always influencing you whether you like it or not, so you'd better get amongst people who influence you in a positive way or like I said, have some alone time right now as you get your racing where you want it to be.

What you watch and listen to

I also saw a big shift in my attitude and life when I started to fill my head with the kind of entertainment and information that helped me improve my mind and my skills.

As you may know I am a huge Rocky fan. Even though Rocky is a fictional character, he still portrays the very values that I hold dear to me. The values of progress, personal growth, challenge, creating a life better than what you start with and perseverance.

The true story of how Sylvester Stallone created Rocky the film and his personal journey is wrapped up in that film and that always gets me going. Let alone the soundtrack.

The Rocky soundtrack has always been just a click away for most of my life and it has got me up off my backside on the days when I really don't feel like putting in the work.

We can get influenced by movies, music, YouTube videos, podcasts, documentaries and any other form of media. If you fill your head with things that move you and educate you at the same time then this kind of constant mental influence can keep you on track and even help you overcome the other things in your life that may not be in place yet (like your friends or people who are good for you).

Make sure you pay attention to what you purposefully take in via your senses. Whether it is through your eyes or ears, something you watch, listen to or both, just mentally digest the things that will help you become more and get more from yourself.

You are what you take in.

Your environment

Sometimes you can have great friends and you spend time filling your head with the best content, but I want you to also make sure that your environment is also serving you.

If you are living in a household where there is a lot of negativity, arguing or if it is preventing you from working as you need to then you can do one of two things. You can either move out and change your living arrangements or you can translate things and let this crap hole motivate you to create the career that will help you escape.

If you live in an area where you find it hard to go to the gym or work on your career, then do what you can to move and make your life more efficient. Even if you are in a country where motorsport isn't available, then it's time to see how you can move closer to where motorsport is easier to gain access to.

Just like a wannabe actor does when they are trying to break into Hollywood, they go to Hollywood. Same for racers.

Your environment matters. It is hard enough to become and remain a professional race driver as it is, there is no need to make it even harder by living in a place or an environment that makes it even harder.

This is about setting up your external life so it serves you. Think about it.

Your internal focus

Finally, a seriously powerful way for us to influence ourselves is by what we play in our mind.

No matter how well you stand at the door of your mind and set up your life externally, if you are regularly replaying memories that sap your self-belief or constantly talk yourself down, then you will effectively be acting as a virus in your Matrix.

What you internally focus on (the pictures, movies and self-talk that you play in your mind) is what you experience. Things can be going well with your career and you may be advancing but if you are toxic on the inside then this will eat away at you.

Take on the responsibility to once again be your biggest fan.

Nobody in this world will support you like you can support yourself. You are your number one priority so treat yourself that way. Take care of yourself and what you mentally spend time on.

I would much rather you master this part compared to everything else we have spoken about in this chapter. If you have degenerate friends, watch brain numbing movies all the time and live in a pit, but your mind is set up in a way that supports you, then that is better than the other way round.

Start to notice how you talk to yourself, especially at critical times when you make mistakes or do not meet your expectations. If you are putting yourself down by making comments like "I always mess up", "I am just no good at this" or other self talk that is just your frustration beating you up, then take note and interrupt that kind of inner chatter.

Back yourself and allow yourself to perform well. Once again, you are the only real person you have. You need to be your super fan and encourage growth. This doesn't mean that you should go around being big headed here, you just need to be your own coach and help yourself through this. You are all you have.

Summary

Most of what we covered here is conscious mental conditioning. These are life and habit alterations that give you the best chance of helping you thrive.

Make sure that you keep an eye and ear out for what is influencing you and use PWA to help you. Feed your mind with the influences that will advance your warrior mind so you automatically improve as you go through each day.

Your mental diet is as important as any other diet, you need a fit mind. Feed and exercise it well.

Training Exercise – Your Influences

This is the easiest training exercise of all, all you need to do is open up your WM Workbook and in the designated areas write out the kind of people, music, films, books and other information that you are going to use to influence you and keep you growing as a person.

Once done, move on to the last chapter of Part 3 where we hit your emotions.

Master Your Emotions

CHAPTER EIGHTEEN

Master Your Emotions

"Everything negative – pressure, challenges – are all an opportunity for me to rise"
Kobe Bryant

To finish the Training Camp off, I want to divert your mind to the all-important subject of your emotions.

When you mention the word 'emotion' to a race driver, they often presume that you are referring to the emotions they feel when crossing the line in first place or when they are angry at someone in a race.

These are times when you experience emotions but in this program when we talk about emotions we are referring to your emotional state. The emotional state that you are in at any given time creates your overall mood, mindset and mental mode that you are in.

As a driver, just like a warrior, you need to be able to manage your emotions and state of mind.

If your mind had a North Star of its own then it would be to fully master its emotions and for it to create whatever mood it wants, when it wants it. That is the true North Star here.

This is the kind of pursuit that I have been on and what I want you to work on as you go through life.

Emotions playing a key role

Drivers often have an unwanted passenger in the car with them, that passenger is their mindset. They are carrying certain emotions within them at critical times and in doing so they make unforced errors in the car or fail to get the best from themselves.

Here are some examples of how drivers let emotions affect their performance:

1. Let's take a look at a driver who is starting from pole. This driver executed well in qualifying and earned their right to start at the front of the grid, they have shown that they genuinely have the speed. Yet a driver in this position can still be full of self-doubt and anxiety. He may be nervous because he has messed up most of his previous race starts and does not want to do it again. He knows it is a big issue, his Dad is constantly reminding him of how bad he is at race starts. Due to him focusing on the his unsuccessful starts he becomes tense and emotionally out of control. This can cause him to mess the start up again and further amplify the problem.

2. Another driver is in qualifying, she feels as though she is driving well, but her lap times are not competitive. She then panics, worries about what people will be thinking and then starts to make mistakes. This causes her to come into the pits angrily shouting about the car and blaming others.

3. Another driver is losing time at the fast corner that has little runoff area and is known for being a dangerous corner. His fear of crashing is causing him to brake too much going into the corner. The driver can then never be competitive that weekend.

4. Our last example is of a driver who is being caught by another car in the race, each lap the car behind is getting closer until they are filling the mirrors. The lead driver becomes stressed due to the amount of worry they have for losing their position. He then starts to over-defend and makes himself vulnerable. In contrast, the attacking driver sees this and starts to grow more in confidence and quickly executes an overtaking manoeuvrer. With that confidence the attacking driver pulls away whilst the other driver is left mentally beating themselves up and frustrated.

These are just a few examples of how we often see drivers letting their emotions build a mindset that brings them down. You will see these kinds of situations and scenarios playing out in every single race.

Most of my coaching is in this area because I fully believe that this is one of the most important areas to master as a driver. On top of it serving you when racing, if you can get a hold of your emotions then it will help you in every part of your life.

You can have all the speed and driving skills of a world champion but if you cannot execute or if you are easily beaten due to your emotions, then you will get nowhere.

We are walking emotion factories

As humans we have a full spectrum of emotions available to us. We can go from moment to moment feeling excited, scared, curious, calm, anxious, angry, happy, empathetic, frustrated, hopeful, loving, elated, relaxed or depressed. To name a few.

We have these emotions at our disposal, and they can be accessed at any time, yet most people overlook the importance of mastering how they use their emotions.

Most people are victims of their emotions and get pushed around by them.

Another belief that I think will help you is:

I am the one who is responsible for creating the emotions I want!

If you think back to what I said about people having different reactions to the same event in life due to their perspective (the way they see and translate things), then I want you to consider this as being the same.

225

Some of the emotions we feel seem automatic and we have certain external triggers that fire our auto responses but as easily as these emotions were programmed in the first place, we can 'reprogram' ourselves to feel and attach new emotions to things.

It is my belief, and from what I have experienced I believe this to be true, that on the whole we can virtually control our emotions and produce the ones we want when we need them.

You will have had times when you went from angry to happy, when your friend told you some bad news, but then they shouted "Syke", and you realised that they were just joking.

Or how you feel severely stressed in a race as you are trying to hold onto your lead whilst P2 is attacking at every corner, and then just one lap later you immediately feel elation when you cross the line first and take the win.

That is two opposite emotions that you shifted between in the short amount of time it took you to exit the last corner to crossing the line. Quite impressive how you produced two emotions in such a short space of time.

You have done this kind of thing all of your life, you are already a master at producing emotions and skipping from one to the other depending on what you are focusing on.

You will even do it consciously sometimes, you will notice that you want to feel more motivated or up for a fight, so you stick on some music to get you mentally there. Even though that song is two minutes long, you will already be feeling the effects of it after the first ten seconds.

I see humans as walking emotion factories. We produce emotions that we want due to what we pay attention to, how we translate things and how we hold our body (breathing, muscle tension, posture, etc), then in turn these emotions produce actual chemicals that flood our body.

Try it

An exercise that you will hear me talk about a lot is referred to as the 'Person behind the door' and it goes something like this.

If there is a door nearby you now, I want you to pretend that there is a person behind that door and by me telling you what emotion that person is in, you will be able to tell me what kind of thing they are thinking about and how they are holding themselves physically.

If there isn't a door nearby then just imagine there is, and there is a person behind it that you cannot see.

So, imagine that the person behind the door is sitting in a chair and is feeling depressed and is incredibly sad right now.

Just picture them for a few seconds.

What is their posture like, are they sitting bolt upright with a straight spine or slumped in the chair?

Are their shoulders high up or rounded?

Is their chin raised up with a beaming smile on their face or are they looking downward to the floor with a blank facial expression?

Are they breathing full and fast, or are they breathing slowly?

Every time I have asked people this over the past twenty years or so they have always said that the depressed person behind the door will be slumped in the chair with rounded shoulders, their head will be down, they will have a sad or blank expression on their face and they will be breathing slowly. They may also be crying.

Then we move on to what they would be thinking about. So I ask you again, what kind of thoughts and self talk would that depressed person be thinking?

What would they be saying to themselves or seeing in their mind?

Would they be thinking, "I am so grateful for my life right now" or would they be saying something like "Why me?".

Would they be picturing past funny moments, or would they be replaying a sad time or worrying time?

I will never belittle anyone who is going through depression, it can be a serious obstacle in someone's life, but for the purpose of me getting my point across I think that once again you will tell me that this certain person is feeling sad because they are playing the kind of thoughts in their mind that create that emotion.

If I were to fall into the habit of holding my body in that slumped, head down and slow breathing way. Then on top of that I started to focus on all the things that are not perfect in my life and like a scratched record I would say things like "Why me?" and "Life is shit" then I too would quite quickly produce the same emotions.

Give it a go, you can play with your mind and body to create all sorts of emotions. That is the essence of what we are talking about here.

Your brain is always watching you

The way I like to make people think about this is to tell them that their brain is always watching them. Your brain looks upon you waiting for you to give it some signals. If you sit in the chair like this person and think constant negative thoughts, it will then say "Oh ok, you want that emotion...here you go".

It will then instantly hand you sadness, regret or similar emotions that it thinks you are trying to access.

Your mind is constantly looking for what you are thinking and how you are holding your body.

If you start to think of the good times you had with your loved one's last night, and it can see that you have a smile on your face, it will say "Ok, here is the emotion that goes along with that combination" and it will produce the feeling love, happiness, humour or gratitude.

You have many thought and body combinations that you have learned in your life and you have associated them with emotions. So when you pull an emotional combo then your mind obliges. It is like providing the ingredients for a cocktail.

Back to the 'person behind the door' exercise again, if I was to tell you that behind the door this time is a super excited person who has just won the lottery jackpot, I think you can tell me how they would be sitting in the chair.

Actually they would probably be standing on the chair and jumping off it with joy.

You would easily be able to tell me what kind of facial expression and breathing they would have. Plus what kinds of things they would be thinking.

Yes they have the external stimulus of winning the lottery, but still the emotions they created because of it still have a mental focus and body expression that goes along with them feeling ecstatic. They will pull these mental and physiological triggers each time they want to feel ecstatic. It will be their 'go to' combo and the brain will produce the emotion they want to feel.

Mind and Body

One of the quickest ways to produce a certain emotion is to hold your body (physiology) and create the thoughts that are aligned with that emotion, then the emotion that corresponds to this combination will be produced.

Hollywood and moviemakers understood the importance of this a long time ago and know full well how to produce emotions within people who watch their movies. By what they show you on screen, by the music they play and with the storyline they can virtually lead you to focus on certain things in your minds and even influence your physiology to create certain emotions that they want you to feel.

If you watch an audience who are watching a scary film, compared to an audience watching a romcom, you can see the physiological differences. In both types of movies the couples in the audience may be holding each other, but they will be holding each other in very different ways depending on the type of movie

I purposely use the Mind and Body technique to produce certain emotions.

If I want to be instantly confident, before standing up to speak or going to meet a client, I will firstly snap myself into a confident stance or sitting position if I am sat down. My chin will go up. I will breathe fully, put a smile on my face and slightly puff my chest out. My jaw will be slightly tense along with certain muscles. When I pull this body position my mind already knows that "It's game time".

I will then say something in my mind that backs me up, I may focus on delivering maximum value to the person or people I am about to speak to. I may bust a move and say something out loud.

I will quickly visualize a glimpse of the great time we are about to have and within a second or two I will have produced the emotion called confidence.

If I were not to do this, and instead I was to focus and remember times when things did not go to plan and have the physiology that was more representative of a scared mouse, then the brain would go into protective mode and would produce an emotion that would be the opposite to confidence. I might feel worried or fearful of the meeting or speaking gig not going to plan.

This is how simple it can be to produce the mindset and emotions you want, and once you practice this then it is much more than just a mental patch, it becomes super reliable and more long term.

It becomes automatic.

Emotions can be signs

This emotional flexibility and management can take you a long way and can help you show up mentally when you most need to, but I want to make sure that you do not ignore the automatic emotions that you feel.

Our minds use emotions as warning signals to communicate to us. When we have a gut feeling about something or when we have an emotion pop up, it can often be our inner intelligence warning us that we need to take action. These automatic emotions should never be ignored. They should be initially listened to and it's up to you to decide what to do with that emotion, either take it as a sign for action or change it if it is of no use.

If you are working hard and you begin to feel overwhelmed, then this could be your mind sending you an emotion to warn you. It may be telling you to either get assistance from someone who can share the workload or that it is simply time to take a break.

If you start to feel mild depression on a fairly consistent basis then this could be your brain's way of telling you to resolve something and no longer ignore it.

If you feel alone, then this could be your brain telling you that you had better get out and reconnect with friends or family, or meet someone to share your life with.

If you are feeling nervous about an upcoming event then this could be your mind telling you to prepare for the event more. Deep down it may know that you haven't put the required preparation in so it's time to do that.

If you are feeling guilty about not seeing your partner due to the amount of time you are spending on your craft, then take note, you may just need to put your work down for today and spend time with your loved one.

So even though it is important for us to produce the emotions we want when we want them, on the other side of that we must also listen to the emotions that are automatically produced because it may be our mind's way of communicating something to us.

It may be a trapped emotion from the past that needs to be released or it may be your mind reminding you to deal with something that is coming up. Either way, listen to it, see if it is valid and decide if you need to change something or change the emotion itself.

Emotional exercising

Like everything else you do, to get this down and to produce the emotions you want will take a bit of practice because you have done it your whole life without thinking about it. Now that you want to take control of this area you will have to do this quite a few times before you get really good at it, before you can create emotions on demand.

The exercises attached to this chapter are to help you practice this emotional management.

I will run you through an exercise that I want you to do regularly. At some point of the day I want you to go from one emotion, to another. I want you to train yourself to change your emotions when you want to.

If you notice that you are feeling bored at home one day, and you want to feel motivated, then take it upon yourself to produce that emotion as quickly as you possibly can.

If you do this often, then over a short period of time you will show your mind who is in control and you will demonstrate your ability to create certain emotions on demand. Eventually you will get this down and it will be something that will separate you from all the other drivers out there.

The exercise

What we will do is jump from emotion to emotion so you can start to train yourself.

First off, let's get sad.

Think like you would and sit/stand as you would if you wanted to feel sad.

- Lower your chin
- Slightly tilt your head

- Relax the edges of your mouth
- Slow down your breathing
- Put that sad look on your face without forcing it
- Think of a sad moment from your past
- Make a small sighing noise

If done thoroughly you will be feeling the sadness coming on.

Remember that this is just created, and you can change it anytime you want. It is not real.

Once there and feeling genuinely sad, I want you to radically change your focus and physiology to create the emotion...happiness.

Do this:

- Think of a memory or something that instantly puts a smile on your face
- Then put that big beaming smile on your face
- Sit in a way that a happy person would
- Replay that happy thought in your mind
- See it and hear everything that was going on then

Oh it was a great time.

Boom, there is happiness.

Once there I want you to shift into feeling motivated. Do this by:

- Think the thoughts that get you pumped
- Think of your racing goal

- Sit or stand as you would if you were ready to go into a fight and you can't wait to get going
- Get your chin up
- Have a strong looking facial expression
- Breathe in deeply
- As you breath out think again about your dream goal with a slight smile on your face
- Stand like a superhero

There you go, you are ready to rock.

I want you to keep playing with this.

Come up with as many emotions as you can back-to-back and prove that you can jump from one emotion to another.

When you want to produce the emotions you want, then just know that you can do this anytime you.

You are the boss.

The main takeaways

The main things to remember when it comes to your emotions is that you have more control over them than you might think.

Emotions are extremely useful because they are the mind's way of communicating to us, but as an athlete who needs to perform on demand, so you need to possess the skill of creating the emotions you want when you want them.

As a Warrior, you don't always get to pick when you go to battle, the race calendar is set by someone else, that potential sponsor may walk into the room when you least expect it, so you need to create the required mindset at short notice.

You will be thrown many challenges when the only thing that will pull you through is by you being in the correct mindset.

Due to you living a life like this, you have no choice but to have the ability to create the emotions and mental states you need.

Practice this and remember the equation that creates an emotion, it is...

What you focus on + How you hold your body = The emotion

The end of Part 3

I will teach you some of my favourite techniques for managing your emotions throughout the next part of the book. One to look out for is the ABC technique, it is a useful one for changing emotions whilst on the go.

For now, this is the end of Part 3 of the Warrior's Mind, next we will enter the battlefield.

PART 4
On The Battlefield

CHAPTER NINETEEN

The Battlefield

> "*The most important 6 inches on the battlefield is between your ears*"
> *Jim Mattis*

Welcome to the battlefield. You made it to the final part of the Warriors Mind. So far you have dug out the foundations and have built the framework of your Matrix.

Now we are moving on to the specific mental strategies that can be used to help you overcome the kind of challenges that you face on a race weekend and as you compete throughout the season.

Here's what is in Part 4:

Chapter 20 - Be a leader. Great warriors make great leaders. Leaders of their army (team) and leaders of their own mind. We will kick this part of the book off with this important skill.

Chapter 21 - Prime your Warrior Mind. We will go through the process of how you can win each day that you go to battle, whether at home or at the track. How to set the mind up so you do show up and work as you need to.

Chapter 22 - Prepare for a race weekend. Here I will share some effective tips for how best to prepare for a race weekend.

Chapter 23 – Visualization. This is an important skill to help with your preparation as well as your mental training.

Chapter 24 - Handle fear & your nerves. After visualization we will talk about fear and nerves because performance anxiety and getting nervous before a race is a common thing that you will need to deal with. In this chapter we will cover techniques to help with this.

Chapter 25 - Performing in qualifying. No need to over describe this one. Qualifying is your time to shine so you need to set things up correctly for this session and execute well.

Chapter 26 - Maintain concentration - The mindset for races. Maintaining concentration really means that you have the ideal mindset for a whole race.

Chapter 27 - Handling teammates, jealousy and criticism. All three of these topics can be overcome with your ability to handle people and their actions. Another important area.

Chapter 28 - Get back on that horse. The final main chapter is for times when you have lost your mojo and if you've hit a rough patch. We will also talk about motivation in this chapter.

Chapter 29 - The Identity Split. There is always room for one more mental training technique. Here we use Identity Coaching to unearth how you have been mentally operating whilst at your best and at your worst. You need to know this.

We are going to hit the most vital areas that you must master if you are to achieve victory whilst on your battlefield. We will also cover how to overcome mistakes, how to handle pressure and how you can inspire others.

Be The Leader

CHAPTER TWENTY

Be The Leader

> ## "
>
> *"Earn your leadership every day"*
> *Michael Jordan*

How can we acquire the Warrior's Mind without shining the spotlight of importance of your ability to be a leader?

You need to lead races, lead your race team, lead your personal team of people that are helping you (your army), lead your career and lead your way to your North Star.

Without you steering the ship and guiding all these factors then you run the risk of drifting away from what's important to you and not being in control of your destiny.

You care about you and your career more than anyone else could ever do because quite simply, it's your life and your main priority. It's on your mind 247. So who better to make sure that things get done than you?

Your dream is your dream, it is your responsibility.

People may come and go, it may be important to them for a certain period but they have their own lives to lead but for you it is a lifetime commitment. It's your baby.

If you lack the people skills, the sales skills, the persuasion skills and leadership skills required to keep you on course then you're going to add yourself to the already overpopulated pile of washed-up drivers.

You should see your racing as a company, where you are the CEO. You are the person who makes the decisions and who must put in the work for anything to happen.

You are on the front line

Picture a battle scene with two opposing armies standing opposite each other at each end of the battlefield. The warriors are all stood there poised and ready for the command to charge.

Well, you are on the front line of one of those armies and about to lead your troops into hand-to-hand battle.

This is the battle equivalent to what you are facing with your racing, you can view your army that stands beside and behind you as the people who are with you in your career.

This may be your family, your race team, your close friends, your management, your coaches, your sponsors and anyone else who could be in your clan.

As the warrior who this means the most to, you have taken the role as the leader of your army, the commander who must direct things and give the orders.

If you're the kind of driver that turns up to a race circuit and just does as they're told, who doesn't really make an impact, drives the car fairly well and is relatively invisible then that's no good. That's not a champion. That's not a warrior.

It is not your job to blend into the background and not be noticed, your racing cannot afford that allusiveness and lack of direction. You need to be the person that people listen to and will go that extra mile for.

The warrior is the individual who inspires the team, the warrior is the person who can get the team to work harder for them and is a person who gets noticed as they fight their way to the top.

If you are young, if you are still a teenager or in your early twenties, then you need to have the ability to lead a team of mechanics and engineers who are in their 30's, 40's, 50's and older.

Believe it or not, even when you are young you are still practically the boss in your race team. You pay towards the wages of everyone there, or if not then you need to be valuable to your race team through your results. Either way, you play a major role in the team.

Your behaviour is contagious

How you act, the emotions that you display and your work ethic are all witnessed and taken in by your team members. They then react to this and your behaviour has a big influence on their behaviour.

You will see a big difference within the team's working environment depending on how a driver behaves. If the driver always needs to be encouraged to make sure he or she is working like they should, or if the driver is often miserable and not inspiring, then the team will quickly lose the drive and motivation to work as they should be.

If however the driver turns up each day with an impressive attitude and work ethic, then this seriously motivates the team and they naturally raise their own standards. They will then go that extra mile for their driver.

If you only give 60% effort then they will only give 60% effort. That goes for your management, your coaching staff and everyone else who is with you. This is something that a lot of drivers do not realise and it is something you've got to learn as fast as possible if you want to succeed.

If you ignore this, then it won't be long until a teammate steps up to that leadership role and has the team wrapped around their little finger.

Be disciplined

Self-discipline is a common trait of top warriors and leaders.

Your discipline can be seen from the outside when you show up on time at the track, by how you work and if you follow through on the things you actually say that you are going to do. Discipline can even be seen when you fill out your feedback form each time. These kinds of things show that you have discipline and as a result you not only show your mind that you are a person of your word, but the team sees this and also follow suit.

They are much more likely to follow someone who is outworking them compared to the usual driver they will have experienced up to now.

This is really all about your standards. If you have high standards of what you expect from yourself, and you keep dotting the i's and crossing the t's, the people you work with will feel compelled to do the same to avoid being exposed.

So if you want to be the leader then you must lead by example. Be the way you want the team to be.

When you come back into the paddock after a 'bad' session, it's OK to have a few minutes of feeling sorry for yourself, we all do that because it is just our mind expressing it's disappointment for not meeting its expectations. But after those few minutes, it's up to you to get back into work mode and regain your title of being the leader again.

You can always spot a true leader in the army, in a company or in sport, they are the ones who roll up their sleeves and sort things out when they are most needed.

As everybody else is running away from the danger or when stuff hits the fan, a leader remains centred and comes up with solutions.

You are no different to a fighter in the UFC, when a fighter gets punched square in the face, they can't just curl up in a ball and wish for it to all stop, or complain about how the other fighter isn't being fair or that they weren't quite ready. If you do this in a fight then it will only be a matter of seconds before the next hit is coming and this time it might be a knockout punch.

The fighter needs to quickly come up with a solution and figure out how they can overcome the situation they are in. You need that same ability, you compete in a sport where you also must take on what's just happened and quickly adjust and come up with the best answers on the spot.

Thinking resourcefully whilst in the heat of battle is when a leader is in their element and it's what a top driver needs to be good at.

I want you to make sure that every single time you go to the track, you know that you are the leader. You are the person who says what they want on the car. You are the person who goes through things thoroughly with your engineer and you must know exactly how to drive each corner.

This supports the importance of your knowledge. You need to know what you are talking about and I will say it again, you must be a master of your craft.

Everything is your fault

When you become the leader you are also the one who takes the blame for everything.

If the team miscalculates something you take it on as your fault for not giving them the right information or spotting it yourself.

If your engineer or mechanic makes a mistake, you put it on you because you didn't help them create the mindset they needed to be in.

This sounds like a mental burden but this is a better way to control your environment and to have more of a say in your life.

This kind of responsibility is not for everyone, but neither is the role of being the leader.

You will hear many people say that they want to be an F1 driver or they want to own their own billion-dollar company, that's great, but they fail to understand that to do those things successfully they must excel in certain areas. You cannot achieve the goal you want just because you want it more than most.

That's why true champions do not come round that often. However, if you are the kind of person to pick up this book and you have the goals that you have, then I have confidence that you can fill this role if you **completely dedicate yourself and remain self-aware.**

Heck you need to if you want to get that North Star, you have no choice. You are the boss.

There is a fine line between being the boss and being bossy, but if you just lead by example then you will find the right balance.

Ayrton Senna

Ayrton Senna was known for being hard on his teams, he used to look over his mechanic's shoulders checking the tyre pressures they were putting in and wanted to know everything.

This wasn't to intimidate anyone this was him just doing what he could to maximize and control as much as he could. He was hard on the team but they allowed for it because they could see how hard he was on himself. His standards were through the roof.

He brought such a high level of work ethic so the team couldn't complain when he expected them to do the same. So they did.

These are the kinds of drivers to learn from.

They didn't do everything perfectly but they have certain attributes that are useful when forging a career in motorsport. Leadership is often one of those attributes that you can adopt from them.

If you take on all the responsibility, take on all the lessons, think about how you want to win the day and communicate it to your team (and you communicate this in the right way) then you will be leading the team before you know it.

They will soon be looking at you for the answers.

Study leadership

I want you to study leadership. Read books, watch documentaries, get audiobooks and watch video clips of leaders to mentally digest how these people did what they did and how they got a team of people to work for them.

People like Nelson Mandela, Michael Jordan, Winston Churchill, Alex Ferguson and even warriors like Alexander the Great.

In reading, watching and listening about these individuals who achieved so much, you start to pick up the things that link them and you pick up personal traits that will help you in your career.

Most drivers don't know how to lead, they are treading on people's toes all the time, the teams are talking them down behind their back and nobody is really motivated to help these drivers, unless they are being paid to be there.

Do not let that be you, be that driver that stands out because of the leader that you are.

Be the boss so when you arrive and speak up, they listen.

When you work, they work to keep up.

Have the emotional control that causes you to be the one who is still mentally present when everyone else is freaking out.

Make this yet another study that you never stop with and make it another part of your game that separates you from other drivers.

Jules

Over my time in this sport I have come across a few drivers who really know how to lead their team. One of them that really stands out for me was Jules Bianchi.

When he came and joined our team in World Series Formula Renault 3.5, he turned up with a good reputation because he had been doing well in GP2 for a couple of years and it was clear that he was on his way to F1.

When he came to the team, he had such respect from the team members because you could just tell that he was there to do the business.

He was treating it like it was his last chance to prove himself (which it may have been) and he was determined to give it his all.

This was evident because he would always be working in the team truck until late, he was fully focused in the debriefs, he was talking to all team members and he was deep into the details of his driving. He was just there to work.

He was very polite and not rude to anyone, but he had a fire within him and he was there for one reason and one reason only...to do what he could to win.

He wasn't the quickest driver in the Formula Renault 3.5 car to start with but due to his dedication he constantly improved and would have won the title if he hadn't gotten taken out in the last race of the season.

When a team sees that kind of application and dedication they want that driver to win and want to be a part of that goal.

Please take this example of how Jules was, as an insight and as a reminder for what it takes.

Prime Your Warrior Mind

CHAPTER TWENTY-ONE

Prime Your Warrior Mind

> **"**
>
> *"I stay ready, so I don't have to get ready"*
> *Conor McGregor*

Race drivers, like warriors, need to constantly prepare themselves for what is about to come.

You are either debriefing from what has just happened or you are preparing for your next event but for us in this program, I want to focus on three different types of events that you have to mentally prepare for.

They are:

1. How to prepare for a working day (this chapter)
2. How to prepare for a race weekend (chapter 22)
3. How to prepare for a qualifying session or race (chapter 24)

To keep things targeted, these three events to prepare for are split over three chapters.

For now, I want to show you how to mentally prime yourself so you can create the warrior mindset needed to help you crush your days.

To create a Warrior's Mind then you can't just expect to train it whilst on race weekends. Oh no, you need to condition it over time so it becomes your new default mental setting and is automatic when racing. All the hard work is done away from the track.

This means that you need to activate your warrior mindset each and every day. Having the Warrior's Mind isn't just a pick up and put down mental technique, it is a way of life and a way of living for you. As with a normal muscle in your body, your mind needs to be exercised and built over time so it grows into what you want.

Being a racing driver you should be super busy on the days that you are at home. These are the days when you've got to go and find new sponsors, liaise with your current sponsors, keep fit, work on your branding, speak with your team and management, do coaching sessions and train on the simulator.

If you are also holding down a job, are still at school or have a family then you need to fit all of this in around these commitments. A driver's life is full.

If not and you find yourself with too much time on your hands, then it's time to get busy. You need to get rid of that white space on your calendar and treat your racing like a full time job. A warrior doesn't train part time, they make it their life purpose.

It is not your job to sit at home playing Call Of Duty all day, instead you should be answering this question "How can I train myself in sport specific areas whilst at home and grow my career today?".

Then you spend your days answering that question through your actions.

That should be your fascination. You should always be asking "How can I improve myself when I'm not in the car?"

The mindset to do this

To make sure that you show up each day and blast through your racing career To Do List, just like any entrepreneur has to, it helps if you actively create the mindset of the person who could crush each day.

To help you to this I want to share with you a priming technique that I have used for many years and it is one of the most important techniques within this book.

I had to learn this early on because I have worked at home for some time now and when you do that you can easily become distracted or not really be in the correct work mode throughout the day.

When I learned how to prime my mind and kick it into action on demand, I took this on and it has been one of my secret weapons ever since.

When at home I will be either be eCoaching clients, organising my business travel plans, writing a book (like this one you're reading now), doing podcasts, recording the race driver coach show, planning driver's training schedules, sim training with drivers, talking with teams, career advising, working on my own branding or I am running the company.

To make sure that I am at my best and execute as I need to, I create the mindset needed first, then I throw myself into it. I prime my mind so it is set up correctly for each current day's goal.

Mental priming is something that can help people completely change their lives and massively improve their performance. So I want to share this priming routine with you so you can experience rewards that it offers.

For the rest of this chapter I will run you through the exact mental priming routine that I personally do. Feel free to modify it so it fits with you.

The Morning Priming Routine

I usually spend around ten minutes on this but the priming routine I am about to share with you can be done in as little as five minutes if you need to.

To give you the full rundown on how I prime my mind and the mind of my drivers to get them battle ready, I will walk you through the whole process from start to finish so you can replicate it and adjust it to suit you.

Prepare your music

To prepare for this, I suggest that you have a playlist put together for you to listen to whilst you are priming your mind. If you are on

Spotify then the actual playlist that I use for my priming is on my public playlist called Priming Run.

Feel free to find me on Spotify and use my playlist as you prime for your day, it will be like we are doing it together.

From time to time I change the songs but at the moment of writing this book, my playlist looks like this:

Track 1 - Intro by The xx
Track 2 - We Are Designers by Jacob Shea
Track 3 - No Easy Way Out by Robert Tepper
Track 4 - Champion by Zayde Wolf

Then after these I have a bunch of songs lined up for the times when I want to jog for a bit longer or if I just feel like mixing things up.

As you can see, this is a short playlist and that goes to show how quickly the priming technique can be done. It would be even quicker but I want to make sure that I do some exercise as well during this period so it is longer due to this.

If you choose your own playlist then the basic structure I use is to have the following:

1st song - To be ambient
2nd song - Chillout or classical
3rd song - To be good for working out to
4th song - To be motivational and cause you to feel powerful

These then form the background music for each phase of my priming session.

The 5 Steps

Once you have your preferred music in place, then here is the five step priming process that will help you create the warrior mindset for the start of your day.

This process is best done in the morning but can actually be done any time in the day and whenever you feel like you need to get your mind focused again. The objective is to break you out of your current mood and put you in a state of mind that will help you act as you need to.

So if you are doing this first thing in the morning then the goal is to be up and outside within the first five minutes of you waking up.

Ideally this is to be done before you even look at your messages, emails or scroll through any social media. This process is much more effective if you just get up, go to the toilet, down a small glass of water, then go, before the outside world can distract you.

When you are outside it's time to hit the play button and get going.

A note for all morning scrollers

When I tell people about this morning routine they often react with "But I must check my phone to see if I have missed anything or if there are any emergencies".

If this is the case with you then all you do is set your alarm ten minutes earlier than when you would normally set it and do your priming in under ten minutes.

So by the time you have done your priming routine you will be back for the same time that you would have normally woke up. Then you can check them.

Problem solved for all the message checking junkies out there.

Step 1 - Breathing

Whilst listening to your first music track which can be ambient and just ease you into things, I want you to do a breathing exercise as you walk.

It is a very simple breathing exercise where you breathe in and out using deep diaphragmatic breaths through your nose. Your goal here is to simply breathe in and out in a controlled manner and fill yourself full of oxygen and start to flush your mind and body.

Continue to walk filling those lungs for the entirety of the first song.

Step 2 - Gratitude

When your second song kicks in, it's time to spend a few minutes reminding yourself of the things that you are grateful for in life.

Start with a few parts of your body or senses that you are grateful for, then move out to people in your life that you are thankful for, then finally move out to more global things that you are grateful for.

Here are the kind of things I say to myself if I am doing this on the beach:

"I am so grateful for my heart that beats away every second of the day without me asking it to. I am so grateful for my lungs that breathe in the oxygen that keeps me alive. Thank you for my sight that enables me to see this beach this morning, I am so grateful for my hearing that allows me to hear the waves crashing and for my sense of smell so that I can smell this fresh sea air."

Then I move on to the people in my life, *"I am so grateful for my wife who makes me the happiest man in the world and is so precious to me. I am so grateful for my family who love me unconditionally, I am so grateful to all those who I love and who love me".*

This changes quite often because I may name certain people.

After this I move on to more global things and may say something like *"I am so grateful for this one chance that I have of life, thank you for this opportunity to be alive and for this experience. I am so lucky to be here."* As I do this I may be looking up at the sky to whoever or whatever it may concern.

All of this gratitude part will be done with a slight smile on my face, with my chin up and breathing full. Each time I remind myself of what I am grateful for I feel more at peace and happier as I walk.

By now you are already leaving the stress of yesterday behind and your mind will be resetting itself because it has been reminded of the real truths. When you are in a truly grateful state of mind it is very hard for stress, sadness and anxiety to creep in.

This is the kind of perspective that people have when they are on their deathbed and are advising others. They usually advise people to love more and to live life more. This is our way of suggesting this to our mind before it is too late.

Step 3 - Exercise

Once you are feeling refreshed and grateful, it's time to add some exercise. I personally prefer a slow jog, just to get the motor running and not to over exert the body. This is your equivalent to warming up your engine.

My Rocky music or other motivational music will now play and I will start to jog and allow the mind to think about what today is all about and what I would like to achieve today. It may quickly think of yesterday and what I didn't quite manage to accomplish and add that to the current day's goals.

I also think of what I learned yesterday and how that will improve me as a person for today. Whether the previous day was a good day or not, there is always a lesson if you look for it. The worst of days can teach us more than we may initially realise.

Step 4 - Power Walk

Once I am happy with the exercise, which could be just one song if preferred, then I start to walk back home in a strong and confident way listening to the final song.

During this part I will see my day as done, I quickly visualize what the victory scene for that day will look like so the mind can see what I want.

Then it's my mission to create the mindset required (to make that day's victory scene a reality) by the time I get back home. So when I reach the front door of my house I am mentally on fire and have the mindset needed to dominate that day.

This whole process up to now is effectively my Ring Walk.

Step 5 - Get in the shower and crush it

That's it, that's the priming done. Then I will get in the shower and get to it. If you take daily supplements then sink them with some more water and on you go.

In doing this my productivity (especially for the first four hours or so) went from being just OK to being on fire. To the point where I cannot type quick enough when on the computer.

When I compare this to just doing the average wake up routine of waking up - scanning through the phone - making a coffee - roll into the office, then it isn't even comparable.

I prioritise having the ability to think of an action then immediately executing on it (think - do) because you don't always need to have the right mindset in place, sometimes you just have to get on with things whether you feel like it or not.

Some days you won't be motivated, but you still need to take the action.

But in saying that, if you spend the time to prime your mind in this way then you will improve your mental fitness and mental health, as well as your physical health. You basically set up yourself up to win that day.

Identity coaching

This is just one part of what I like to call Identity Coaching. That's when you take on the identity of the person you need to be in order to act as you want. So if you want to create the results of a champion in your sport then you must take on the beliefs of and become that champion, have them as your identity way before the goal is even achieved.

This way you are the person who can make it happen and increase your chances of success.

That is what we are doing here, you are making sure that you are the person you want to be by the time you get back home and then you act in line with that mindset.

You go outside initially as a tired person who is begrudgingly walking in the cold, and whilst out there you change who you are, you change your identity and return as a warrior.

Then you set that warrior to task.

That's why this is one of my favourite mental routines to radically change someone's life and work ethic.

Don't break your ankle

Be careful. Back in 2020 I was doing this very routine with Liam Lawson at the Mugello race weekend (we did it before going to the track to prime him) and whilst doing the jogging part, I rolled over my ankle and broke it. So yes, be careful because when you are tired you may not be at your most alert.

Preparing For A Race Event

CHAPTER TWENTY-TWO
Preparing For A Race Event

> *"Humble enough to prepare, confident enough*
> *to perform"*
> Tom Coughlin

You would not be a very good warrior if you didn't know how to prepare and plan for a battle. For you that would mean how to prepare and plan things for a race weekend.

I want to spend some time giving you some mental training tips on race preparation and break down the preparation phase for a race weekend.

When going to a race event under prepared you feel behind the game, it is harder for you to feel on top of things and can easily be left behind or miss obvious details.

So we need to set things up as a warrior would as they prepare for battle, to come up with some simple strategies, some game plans and some ways that you can help yourself succeed over a race weekend before you've even got there.

Skipping training will be the end of you

We are going to talk about your time in between race weekends here so I cannot overlook an important thing that happens in this period. This important part I am referring to, is how drivers often get lazy when it comes to them training important aspects of their 'game'.

All too often drivers procrastinate and do not train hard enough on the things they learned from the previous race weekend and due to this they do not improve themselves as quickly as they could.

High achievers, like everyone else, have days when they don't feel like putting the work in but when you experience this then I would like you to call upon our friend again. Our friend called Pain.

As with everything in this book, we must look at how warriors and fighters deal with these times. Well, they often use pain to get them moving.

A soldier may think something like this:

"There is a man in a cave somewhere right now training themselves on how to kill me. They are busting boulders, studying, sparring, coming up with tactics and learning my weaknesses. One day I will meet that man".

Need I say more?

If this kind of thought doesn't get you out of bed then you may have to resort to electric shock treatment.

This one thought will get a warrior out of bed and make sure that they prepare for the day of reckoning with that man who is training away.

Each time you feel like not putting in the work then create a thought like this that will get you off your backside and give you a reality check.

Information gathering

To begin preparing for an event, the first stage is to launch your campaign for gathering as much information and knowledge as you can.

To start with you overview your previous outing or race weekend. Go over the last weekend and note down the personal performance areas that you were under par with and see if they will form part of your development goals in the next weekend.

This will also give you specific things that you need to train on the sim or in the gym between the two events. There are many ways in which you can improve your skills when you're not in the heat of battle, knowing what to improve helps you come up with creative ways to improve whilst away from the track.

That's the information taken from you on the performance side of things. Next you need to gather as much information as you can on the track, even if you have been there many times before.

You need to know the current race lines in the dry and in the wet. Find out if the track has had a recent surface change, which is quite a big thing nowadays because on the FIA circuits recently changed a lot of the track surfaces and in doing so the wet lines completely changed. They are more like dry lines in some places now and even some of the white lines are grippy in the wet.

Find out all you can about the track and go through it all with your team and/or coach.

Hopefully the team allows you to see them for a 'prep day', or at least sets up a zoom session where you can talk about how you're going to approach the weekend, go through some onboards and discuss the things you both want to try with the car.

Do some simulator work to not only relearn the track but to create the mental muscle for that track. You want to know it so well that you could virtually drive it with your eyes closed.

Your goal is to learn as much as you can and feel 100% comfortable with the track layout and all its driving rules before you go.

When I say driving rules I mean that you need to know where to attack and defend, what the most important corners are, what part of each corner is more important and which corners may be your biggest challenge.

Simplify

Once you have gathered this information it is time to simplify it all down so it is memorable and bite size. Prioritise the things that need to be remembered and give your mind the chance to retain it all so you are not overthinking things when you get to the race weekend.

Maybe there is one main priority, you only have one thing that you want to improve from the previous weekend, then perfect. If it's something like your race starts or even something more global that will improve many areas simultaneously then brilliant, that's a win on that side. That will be your personal performance goal for the weekend.

When I'm preparing for an event with the driver it becomes all about simplifying things down. You do not want to go into a race weekend with ten completely different things to improve because it just won't happen.

Instead start with your huge external goal, which may be to win the race. If so then fine, but let's reverse engineer that goal and bring it down to the process of what needs to be done.

If you then said that it is my raw speed, then we would simplify the circuit down to make it easier for you to improve your lap time.

You look at a track map and identify which corners are the most important for a lap time. Then you spend some time on how best to drive them and the team will work on how best to set the car up for them.

You can keep simplifying further by grouping the corners together by understanding the rules for each important corner and see if there are certain rules for driving that multiple corners share.

For example you could just sum it up by saying *"The most important corners are turns 2, 5, 7 and 11. Two of them require good exits and two of them are all about keeping up the minimum speed".*

Straight away you have made all the technical data into some very simple instructions that will help you remember what needs to be done and when you are in the car struggling for that last bit of time, you will remember the overriding fundamental rules that will offer you the answers that you need.

Silverstone is a brilliant example for this because you nearly have half the circuit being full of high speed corners and the other half being medium and slow speed corners. So you need to adopt the mindset and approach of two different types of drivers in one lap.

Once you understand this you have just started the simplification process of a monster 18 corner circuit. Obviously you will go a little deeper but if you keep simple fundamentals then your racing brain will fill in the gaps whilst on the go.

With less of your mind taken up you are more likely to remember the more detailed information that you studied and can access it better whilst driving if needed. Every driver needs a calm mind if they are to drive at their best, a mind that is focused on something simple and to not have too much mental ballast weighing them down. All of this will help that.

You can practice a lot of this on the simulator before you go to the real circuit.

Separate results and the process

You will have external goals and some pressure on you for getting the result you need. It's your job again to avoid over complicating things so refrain from dwelling over what others may be thinking and the "What if" questions that play out the worst-case scenarios.

For you to keep the Warrior Mind you must take an external goal (a race win, a certain lap time, etc) and reverse engineer it down to the actions that you need to take. Completely focus on the process, not the result.

The undeniable truth about every race weekend is that you need to get the absolute best out of you and the car. If the combination of these two areas is enough, and you have a sprinkling of fortune, then you will cross the line in a good position.

So to simplify that down further, all you need to do is make sure you create the mindset you need, you find out how to best drive each corner and you give the best feedback possible on the car. That's all you need to focus your attention on, everything else can clear off.

I repeat, focus on the process and focus only on the things you can control.

If you prepare with that in mind and major on these things throughout the weekend then you will know that you did everything you could. If it wasn't good enough for the win then you build this into the preparation for the following round and go again.

There doesn't need to be any emotion or pressure attached to it, you just do the work and see what the end results are, then you adjust things going forward. Rinse and repeat this for the whole season and see where you end up.

At the very least you will be able to know that you gave it your best shot and unlike other drivers you didn't let the pressure get to you.

Be content with the truth, if you are not quick enough but you gave it your all and did everything in your control then you should sleep easy.

My overriding words of advice when preparing for an event is to - **Prepare well, simplify things and focus on the process.**

Visualization

CHAPTER TWENTY-THREE

Visualization

> **"**
>
> *"The best simulator has always been in my head"*
>
> *Jack Hawksworth*

I'm a big fan of visualization. It works well for me personally as well as my drivers and has been an important part of mental preparation for sportsmen and women for a very long time.

I want to cover visualization because it is a mental tool that can help you prepare and it can be another way for you to advance without being on track.

People get very frustrated when trying to visualize because they cannot really see anything, so they try but quickly give up because they are not seeing vivid images or movies behind their eyelids.

They then conclude that visualization is not for them and that they cannot do it. You know that isn't true. If you can dream whilst asleep then you can visualize.

When you first start using visualization you most likely won't see anything, you may get a quick flash or sense of an image but as soon as you think "There it is", it will disappear, and you are left staring at the back of your eyelids again.

That is because this is another mental discipline that takes time and needs some practice.

Try this

The best way for me to help you know or understand that you can visualize things is to show you something now.

If safe to do so, please sit in a place where you won't be interrupted and where you can do a closed eye exercise.

When your eyes are closed, I would like you to visualize your front door at home. Imagine that you are facing your front door looking at it from the outside.

When done, come back to this book.

I bet you can nearly see your front door right?

You can imagine it and get a sense of what it looks like. You may even know what colour it is and be able to get a sense of that. You can virtually see or imagine where the handle is, maybe you can see the letterbox or see the glass panels if there are any.

That's visualization.

I know you can't do this exercise at the same time as reading this book, but once you have done that first exercise, I want you to do it again but this time I want you to visualize a memory of yours.

Go back to that racing memory when you won the race or when you were on the podium. Or maybe just a memorable time when you were in the car or racing on track. See what you saw back then and see what you can remember of it.

If you really wanted to get into this then you can do what we did with your past memories and change the submodalities and play with the pictures in your mind. You can start to turn up the colour, the brightness, improve the clarity or focus on certain aspects more.

You can even virtually hear the noises of your chosen moment. Maybe the engine or the people screaming and cheering as you're on the podium.

Pick any object to train this

To practice and get better at this you can pick an object that is in front of you right now, even if it is a computer screen, your phone or something out the window, I want you to look at it. Stare at it for a good ten seconds.

Then after ten seconds close your eyes and picture it in your mind.

Do that for a few seconds, then open your eyes, look at the object again. Take even more details in this time then close your eyes again and see the other details you just noticed. Keep repeating this.

I think you will find that you can nearly see the object when your eyes are closed. This is you training your visualization skills.

Use your imagination

You can really change things up if you use your imagination.

You can do this with everyday objects that may be around you. Let's just say that you have a computer screen in front of you, you can stare at it for ten seconds, then close your eyes.

Picture it in your mind and pretend that you actually go inside that computer screen. You can teleport a smaller version of you into the back of the computer screen where you can take a look around at its internals.

I first learned this when I was on that original mental training course called the Silva Method. We started to look at appliances and imagined going inside to find out what parts might not be working properly.

They also made us go outside to pick a leaf off a tree and bring it back to the room. Once we were all sitting there with our leaves in our hands, each of us looked at the leaf, then closed our eyes and imagined going inside that leaf and having a look around.

It's amazing to think but this simple exercise really worked for me and caused me to believe that I can visualize.

You can use a mixture of visualization and imagination to play out certain scenarios, you can play out a meeting that you are about to have or a race that you are about to start.

Visualize your North Star

You can even use visualization to daydream about your North Star.

If you think about your North Star I bet you can virtually see it in your mind's eye without even closing your eyes.

You can get a sense of what the victory scene that we spoke about earlier.

That's because you think of your big goals often and you have a sense for what it will look like when you are there. Or you have a snapshot in your head of someone who has already achieved it and you think of them, and can virtually see them.

The more often you visit your North Star in your mind and see it playing out the more you'll be compelled to go get it. The brain will see it as possible, it will be experiencing it and it will actually pull you towards it.

If you keep showing your mind what you most want then it will start to make instinctive decisions throughout the day (decisions you may not even be aware of) that take you closer to the future vision that you have.

This goes to show that visualization is important for more than one reason. People call it the Law of Attraction but I just recommend that you visualize your goals and go for it.

If you keep reminding the mind of what you most want in detail and you play with it, then it's bigger in the mind.

Your very own reticular activating system will fire up and it will constantly look out into the world searching for things that will take it closer. When you get good at this then visualization is amazing for your long and short term goals.

If you have a race weekend coming up then use visualization for that.

What is it you want?

Who are you going to be?

How are you going to walk into the team?

How are you going to walk towards that car in the collection area and get in the car with confidence?

You can even visualize something that is happening in about five minutes time, you can watch yourself confidently walking to the car, getting into the car and play the future scene as you want it to go.

Visualization is giving your mind a heads up of what you want to happen and the more you do this the better you get at it. When you are then living out that future situation for real, your mind will tend to act as you previously directed it to when you were visualizing it earlier. It reacts as if it has already been there so it is more relaxed.

Basketball players use visualization all the time, when they are shooting hoops they will visualize the ball going in and will even make the whoosh noise as the basketball brushes the net.

They sometimes anchor their confidence of the ball going in with an audible cue by shouting "Boom" as they take the shot on or when the ball goes in. Then when someone shouts "Boom" to them when they have the ball they will automatically feel the confidence to take the shot on. "Boom" becomes their trigger.

Specifics

You can obviously use visualization to imagine driving a lap.

If you are in your race car ready to hit the track, just take a moment, close your eyes and run through what a good lap would look like.

I know people like to time their visualization laps and try to get it as close to the real lap time as possible but there is no need to put any pressure on this. Just take your time if you want and if you want to go through a certain corner over and over again, rewind, see if from different angles then go for it. This is you doing what works for you.

If you have been instructed to make changes to your driving then show the brain what these corrections will be like. If you have been told that you must brake deeper into the corner then visualize what that would actually feel like, not just what you see, but what you can feel as you go into the corner. Now that you are braking more into the apex you will feel a slightly heavier steering due to the extra load on the front, so do what you can to imagine that feeling.

It is good to mentally rehearse things and luckily for you there are so many different things you can do this with, from first laps to overtaking moves, from meetings to driver changes.

Be Creative

You can get creative with visualization to help you build confidence or to help your mind associate certain feelings to your car.

You can mentally look at your car and imagine that it is lit up like a bright light. It is like a ball of energy so when you step into it you feel energised, light and fast. This bright light of a car helps you feel empowered and indestructible.

You can have a belief come from this that when you are in the car, it's as if you are the warrior who has put on his suit of armour. You can feel stronger and stronger with every tug on your seat belts as you get belted in ready to go.

Your mind reacts well to images and feelings so if you back that up by visualizing such things you can create the emotions you want and attach them to certain things.

If you feel intimidated by the other cars, visualize you going out on track and your car being bigger than everybody else's. All the other cars are smaller just like what happens when you get zapped in Mario Kart.

You know that all these visualizations aren't real but in symbolising these kinds of things to your brain you are helping it feel powerful. This is a lot better than doing what many drivers do who are driven by their self-limiting beliefs and have mental imagery that causes them to lose confidence.

The better you get at this the quirkier ways you can come up with that help you see the world in your own way. In a way that helps you most.

Your own reality distortion field.

Using your imagination in this way is exactly what Albert Einstein was referring to when he talked about the importance of imagination. This is your version of that.

Play with it, be a child again and use it in a way that serves you.

Use visualization to create the emotions you want, to help you try things and to practice what you are about to do.

We are all better the second time we do things, this is your way of helping you use that fact.

Get good at this and use it.

Handle Fear & Your Nerves

CHAPTER TWENTY-FOUR

Handle Fear & Your Nerves

> ## "
> *F.E.A.R.*
>
> *False Evidence Appearing Real*

In the public domain race drivers are regarded as a totally fearless and are seen as people who don't even know what fear is.

So I don't think we even need to cover the subject of fear do we?

Yeah right, if only.

It is clear to see just how many drivers are bricking themselves in the collection area before a race.

They're worried about what might happen. They're worried about screwing up. They're worried about experiencing all of those Avoidance Values that they don't want. They are facing failure and walking the tightrope of fortune that lays in front of them.

This means that drivers often find it difficult to get into the mindset they want. Most drivers will say that they are OK once the light lights go out at the start of a race but I often see that they are still not fully in the right mental mode throughout the first lap.

Their nerves and performance anxiety is not letting them come out the gates as strong as they want to. With us spending the time of helping you create the Warrior's Mind here, I want to make this a strong point for you. I want you to make it a goal of yours that you will come out of the blocks on fire, mentally.

Fear is good

It is totally normal and good to have fear as part of your regular emotions. When you feel fear it is just your mind worrying that it may experience something that it doesn't like.

Fear is another emotion that gets instantly delivered when you start to focus on what could go wrong, on how you may be judged by others and you go down the route of thinking about the worst case scenario.

Then if your physiology, your breathing and your facial expressions portray someone who is fearful, then boom there you go, enjoy that feeling of fear that you just created.

Fear is an emotional neighbour to excitement. It just takes a slight shift in what you translate to yourself and how you hold your body to switch between these two emotions.

Yet drivers rarely take the time to do this, instead they swim in a pit of worry and fear when it comes to qualifying or at race time.

Fear is good because it shows you that you can create emotions on demand and it is actually a handy emotion because it is our warning signal from the mind to tell you that it's 'Go time', or that something is coming that you need to pay attention to.

Most of the time it is something you need to get ready for, like a race of a presentation, it isn't something that should paralyse you and cause you to underperform. It is not life threatening.

Warriors are addicted to fear

Fear is what warrior's live for, it's in their blood and they are at their best when they find themselves within a fearful situation. That's the same for drivers.

You are in a sport where you also have consequences attached to your decisions and where you have to think clearly in situations that would make most people freak out.

You are fighting for positions and for victory in front of the eyes of many so each loss is a public one and can harm your reputation let alone your health.

You have plenty of reasons to feel fear, but as with a warrior, you must thrive when the fear kicks it. It is simply the feeling you get when it is time to get busy and do what you do. Without fear you would be bored.

You would not want it any other way, if racing didn't expose you like this then it would just be like playing a computer game that was set to easy level. Nobody wants to compete in those environments.

Although fear may be something you dislike, just know that as a fighter who happens to use a car instead of boxing gloves you need fear as your best friend and partner as you take on the racing world.

Look at how Mike Tyson's former boxing trainer explained fear...

Fear is the greatest obstacle to learning, but fear is your best friend. Fear is like fire. If you learn to control it, you let it work for you. If you don't learn to control it, it'll destroy you and everything around you.

Fear is a flame, it is fire. If it rages out of control then you will get burned but if you learn how to use it then it will empower you.

Fear should be used to drive you, to motivate you and keep you focused. If you use it for that then you will devastate all those who dare to challenge you. It is hard to beat someone who mentally switches on even more when things get risky and when they face failure.

You will have seen the popular video of Mike Tyson when he is walking to the ring and he talks us through what he is thinking, he says:

I'm scared to death. I'm afraid. I'm afraid of everything. I'm afraid of losing. I'm afraid of being humiliated. But I'm confident. The closer I get to the ring the more confident I get. The closer, the more confident. The closer the more confident I get. All during training I've been afraid of this man. I think this man might be capable of beating me. I've dreamed of him beating me. For that I've always stayed afraid of him. The closer I get to the ring the more confident I get.

Once I'm in the ring I'm a god.

No one could beat me.

Believe it or not Mike Tyson was a fighter who would sometimes be crying with fear before a fight, he would need to be calmed down but when he learned how to use it, he was devastating.

This is what I want for you. Each time you get nervous or anxious about what is coming just remember that fear is only an emotion, it is not something that has a hold of you, it is something that you can control and use. You can translate fear so it helps you. You must do this if you are to be the savage you want to be in racing.

Your racing is far too important for you to overlook this and allow a simple emotion to destroy your chances. You are more than that.

Fear gives you an insight to your values

Your fears and the times when you experience intense nervousness can give you a good insight to the Avoidance Values that you have.

If you are super nervous before a race then you will be feeling this because you are entering yourself into a situation where your worst fear may be realised. If you are avoiding feelings of failure, embarrassment and you think that your significance could take a big hit then your mind will naturally act up and cause you to be alarmed.

If this is the case then just take a moment to understand why that emotion is coming up.

The pre-programmed Target and Avoidance Values are being threatened here so you can start to really understand why you are feeling fear.

You can ask yourself a question to find out why your mind is feeling unsettled, a question like "What am I scared of happening here?" or "What about this situation am I fearful of?".

The answers you give to these questions will most likely point to the surface values to start with, but if you dig a little deeper you will find out what your mind is really fearful of and you will see the Avoidance Values that it doesn't want to experience and the threat of some of your Target Values being taken away.

It's the good old Pain and Pleasure Principle again. If you associate enough pain to a certain situation if it doesn't go to plan, then you will cause the mind to worry and become nervous.

I know that it may seem like we are going in circles here but it just shows you again how related this all is and how again, even your fears, come down to your Matrix and the way you see things.

F.E.A.R - False Evidence Appearing Real

When you are getting into the car for a race or you are just about to step into a boardroom to pitch your sponsorship proposal to a big company, the fear and nervousness that you feel is purely created by your good self.

If in either of these scenarios you do not achieve the results you want, you either come last in the race or they laugh you out of the boardroom, none of these so called failures will result in you losing your life or you getting injured or your loved ones getting hurt in any way.

So apart from what we spoke about with your values, the actual fear and nervousness isn't actually real. There is nothing major to fear here. If you screw up then you lose a race, if you stall on the grid then it's a little embarrassing for a short period but really that's nearly as bad as it can get.

OK you could have an incident and get injured, but very rarely is that the cause for your fear. Your fear will be completely associated with the results you get and you not wanting to mess things up.

Like we already mentioned, if you are focusing on those things then you will create fear and anxiousness. That's natural.

Even though the fear may come in at the same time on a race weekend and you will have emotional triggers that set it off, like when somebody tells you "10 minutes until we get into the car" or you hear the famous German words "Achtung Fahrerlager" to call you up to the collection area, I want you to understand that the fear is totally caused by you.

I would never have believed this when I was in the first few years of my racing because I used to get super nervous. I wouldn't be able to eat on race days and when I sat in the car ready to go you could see how heavy I was breathing through my suit.

But then one day, I literally made a decision that completely changed this. I was sitting on the grid waiting to go, feeling sick with nerves as usual, and I said to myself *"You know what Enzo, this horrible feeling that you are getting right now is something you should make the most of because there will be a time when you don't get to feel this anymore. When you're older and no longer race, you will miss this feeling. Most people don't even get to feel this adrenaline feeling, ever. Make the most of it man, once it's gone it's gone."*

I can't remember if I said this out loud or if I just thought it, but I do remember having a smile on my face at the time.

What did I do here?

Without knowing I did two major things that are done to change your emotions.

Firstly, I translated the situation differently and saw it in a different way by stating that this is a good feeling to have. Then secondly, I changed my physiology by smiling.

Once again it the emotion equation, Focus + Physiology = Emotion.

I bloody did it right there and then and guess what happened? No joke here, I completely forgot about being nervous. I talked my way into feeling differently about the run-up period to races.

From that moment my brain preferred this way of seeing things, if I would start to get slightly nervous I would automatically smile and the nerves would go.

In fact they went a little too much because after a season or so I was so relaxed at the start that I was sometimes late to the collection area. I would say things like "I'll be there in a minute; they won't go anywhere". How cocky was I?

Simulators can help

Going back to False Evidence Appearing Real and to the realisation that you are not scared of anything that is life threatening, this can be proven when you see how nervous people get for online races.

We ran some online championships in the first year of the Covid lockdown in the UK and I used to hear drivers saying that they were more nervous racing in the sim than they were racing in real life. Some of the drivers that said this were high profile drivers.

I think it was because we had many top racers attending and it was televised, but either way here we had people crapping themselves prior to playing a computer game.

Crazy huh?

Many of these drivers were also getting stressed when racing. They had the same mental performance challenges during the online races as they did in real life. Their same demons cropped up.

This goes to show that many drivers care so much about their reputation (significance) and want to avoid being publicly humiliated that it causes them to become super nervous and virtually fearful.

There was one current F1 driver (I won't name and shame him) who nearly joined us but then chickened out because he didn't think he would be quick enough.

It also shows that we really do attach dread and fear to things that cannot really harm us, we fear simply experiencing certain unpleasant emotions.

We will attach fear to situations no matter how menial the activity may be, like playing online computer games.

That's how delicate we are as a species and that's why you must set your values, beliefs and perceptions to fit with the task in hand.

Can you imagine a warrior being afraid to play a computer game?

Neither can I.

This takes me back to the beginning of the book when I talked about the opportunity you have right now. You are competing against drivers that have minds that are easily broken and weak.

If you seriously make it your mission to build a bulletproof mind that will give you the traits of a warrior and you also have speed to go along with it, you will crush them.

Fear and Nervousness

Fear and nervousness are just emotions.

Fear can be used to drive you, to get you motivated and to force you to act if you use it correctly. If you fear the thought of failing at your career and having people say "I told you that you couldn't make it as a driver", then this fear can make you put in the work.

It is totally up to you whether these comments from others will drive you or will cause you to cower away.

Nervousness is an emotion we feel when we are unsure of the outcome that we are just about to create, it is the unknown and when we hope that things go well. This emotion is dealt with externally by preparing better and internally by trusting yourself that you will do the best you can.

Also by understanding that you are a strong individual so can deal with the worst case scenario, you will handle it.

If you focus more on what needs to be done (on the process) rather than the result then your nerves may calm down. This is because you are giving your mind something to focus on, directing it instead of letting it run riot.

First change your perception of the task itself, then focus your mind on what you want it to do, then create the emotion you want.

Practice jumping from one emotion to another when you are on the simulator doing online races. Show your mind who is in control.

When entering online races your goal is to create the mindset you want, not the position you want. Focus on what you need to think about and hold yourself in order to create your optimal state. Then repeat it as many times as you can.

You will always feel some fear, it is an important emotion to have and is completely natural to feel it when it is time to step up in some way.

As a warrior, you feel fear but you act anyway.

Perform In Qualifying

CHAPTER TWENTY-FIVE

Perform In Qualifying

"I don't fold under pressure. Great athletes perform better under pressure, so put pressure on me"
Floyd Mayweather Jr

Qualifying is a time when you absolutely must deliver, no exception.

This is the session where you drive at your best and execute. The car will be at its lightest and its fastest, so should you be.

If you are not performing in qualifying and you are not seriously doing something about it, then you may as well hang your helmet up.

Race drivers are known for being fast drivers, if you cannot go as fast as you can in a session that is designed to let you do that, then what are you doing here?

You leave that pitlane going into qualifying knowing that you are going to give this your all. You are going to reach a limit that may not see you coming back. You leave it all out there and do not allow yourself to come back in the pitlane until you have rung everything out of that opportunity.

Drivers often underperform in qualifying because they put a lot of pressure on themselves or are too lap time focused. This causes them to operate using that defence mentality again.

Qualifying is a full attack session. Ok it needs to be calculated and not driven too aggressively or wild, but it is where you claim your position for the race so you need to get on with it.

I will get into how to improve your qualifying now but remember just how important this session is. If you want to succeed, then it is your job to be better than every other driver in qualifying. This is yet another important quest of yours that you must not forget.

To help you get the best out of your qualifying sessions and to get the best out of you, we will split this chapter into two main sections, they are:

1. Practical advice on how to structure things
2. Mental techniques

For qualifying it takes more than just being in the right mindset on your quickest lap, you also need to set things up so that you have the knowledge and structure in place so you can execute as you want. We will start off with the practical advice.

Practical advice and structure

To start with let's get the absolute basics out of the way. They are worth mentioning because it is often the fundamentals that trip drivers up and just as with your Matrix we always need to start things from a firm base before building up.

Qualifying is no different.

Knowledge about the track

As we covered in the chapter 'Preparing for a Race Event', you need to know exactly which corners are the most important for lap time and prioritise getting your head around them first.

You do not want to be searching for time and still figuring things out in qualifying so first off, I want to remind you to do the prep and have this dealt with before you even get to the race weekend.

This also goes for the wet, study previous video, data or ask others to know what the best lines and driving technique are for that track when it is damp and wet.

It is your job as a driver to have all the knowledge you need about the external battlefield called the race circuit. If you lack this kind of knowledge, then that is on you.

Front-load your weekend

Another practical area that drivers often fall down on is that they are still trying things with their driving when in qualifying. They don't put enough emphasis on ironing out all their driving early enough in the initial free practice session.

If you do not have a free practice session before qualifying then that's fair enough, but if you do then you need to front-load your work so you tick all the boxes before qualifying.

There is nothing worse than going into qualifying still being unsure of anything related to your driving technique.

Make it your responsibility to sort the driving in free practice and have done with it. Make sure that you know how to brake for each corner, know the direction of the wind and how they might affect you, make sure you know how to drive each corner as you need to and you have done your best to do that already in free practice.

Think of it this way, qualifying needs to be you simply repeating your lap from free practice, the one that you nailed already. You have done it once so you can easily do it again.

If over recent race weekends you are behind the game and still do not feel like your knowledge and driving is fully on par by the time you get to qualifying then one of your main goals for the coming weekend will be to shift everything forward.

Pretend and treat your pre-weekend prep as your free practice.

Then pretend and treat your free practice as qualifying.

This will force your mind to make sure that you maximise every minute on the lead up to the weekend and every second you spend on track early in the weekend.

This kind of mindset and urgency to sort things early will structure your approach, your schedule and help you be fully up to your best level when you hit qualifying.

This is simple advice but can often be the unlock when it comes to qualifying, plus it helps you mentally as a side benefit.

If you race in a high-level championship for a works team then the team will already have your run plans set for free practice and they will mostly be for car development rather than your driving. In this case it is even more important for you to have your driving down early on.

You will only get one or two performance laps in so you need to be ready to perform. Prepare for this.

If you are not a professional level driver yet, then this whole way of approaching your practice sessions will be good training for those future days.

Free practice isn't a time to slowly get comfortable, free practice is when you freely practice qualifying.

Make sure the team know you intentions so they can set things up and allow you to take this approach.

You may have brake pads to bed in and race runs to do, that is fine, but make time for your qualifying prep. Make it a priority.

Again use your simulator to practice short qualifying runs and use visualisation before and during the weekend to ingrain what needs to be done with your driving, so when you hit the track your mind knows what it needs to do.

If for some reason you still have to adjust your driving quite a bit in qualifying due to not having practice sessions or you had a loss of track time, then take everything the engineer said to improve and simplify it all down to one or two major corrections that will help you globally.

Your goal is to have the knowledge in place and have a free mind when it comes to qualifying so set things up so that is possible.

Plan your traffic management

You can be mentally on fire, know exactly what to do on the driving side and be more ready than ever but if you are messing about with other cars and not getting clear laps then it will be of no use.

Another thing to sort out in practice is your traffic management.

You need to know the following:

- The gap you need for a clear lap.
- Where on the track to make that gap.
- How best to use slipstream at that track.
- Which drivers are ok to follow and which ones to avoid.

If you have radios then have your coach or your engineer help you manage the traffic and let you know when you are in a good spot.

As with everything here, it will also help you mentally and put you in control more. Also, you need rhythm in qualifying so the more clear laps you get the better you can do that to find that last tenth of a second.

Hide the delta

If you have a big delta time in front of you on your dash and it can distract you then try switching that off whilst on your performance laps. I say this because it can take you out of your flow and destroy your optimal mental zone.

If you are repeatedly reminded how you are doing timewise then you are activating the conscious mind too much and you are going to end up trying to make up too much time in a single corner.

The delta is great for when you are learning the track and trying to understand where to find time in practice or even in a race but when you are in qualifying you need to allow yourself to just go.

To drive one corner at a time and be free, then you can produce magical laps, just like an artist when they are free drawing.

If you are persistently reminded of the result or the current lap time then you can easily become stressed and attach emotional meaning to things.

Try this out first to see if it works for you because some drivers are hooked on their delta or by watching their lap times as they cross the line so you need to get used to trusting your intuition when driving on feel, so give it a go on test days first. This again can be another little mental unlock for drivers.

Not having the delta on doesn't mean that you are showing mental weakness, it is just a way of removing something that could be in your eyeline that is not helping your focus.

Mental techniques

Now that we have addressed some simple practical things for you to do I want to turn our attention to the more mental performance techniques that will help you in qualifying.

Simplify

There is that word again. It goes without saying that you need to chunk down the information that you need to know when going into qualifying. Do not go into this session with mental baggage weighing you down.

You need to be free so if you have a few things to remember then have an easy way of remembering them and remove information that is not vital.

You want to come out of that pit lane and just go. Be a driver and drive the wheels of that thing. It sounds crass but essentially that's how you think when you are mentally on fire.

Once you have all the knowledge, are comfortable with what to do and focus on what's important then you allow yourself to be like this.

That's the first goal for you. It is your goal to feel like this by the time qualifying comes and that is what you want from the very start of race week. Design things so this is possible and let everyone else screw their minds up as they try to cram the learning in late and stressing about the result they may get.

You just go.

Mental warm up

Just like the engine needs to be warmed up before performing, so do you. Have a mental and physical warm up procedure that you do before getting into the car so you can create the mindset you want.

There are numerous things you can do to warm up before a session. Your objective is to focus your mind, create the mindset that serves you best, lightly stretch your muscles and get the blood and oxygen pumping around the body a little more.

This is you getting battle ready and priming yourself.

If you walk down the paddock around thirty minutes before any session starts then you will see an array of drivers bouncing tennis balls, stretching with bands, jumping rope, juggling and even hitting the pads. This is all because they want to snap themselves into fight mode and want to loosen things up.

Your warmup routing is something you should be very comfortable with, something that works well and helps you get into the mindset you want and it is something you should do each time you want to perform.

Singers, actors and obviously athletes all have their routines before going out to perform. Whether they are warming up their vocal cords or doing short sprints, it is all done with the aim to wake up their body and mind.

Some more physical cars require certain muscles to be stretched and warmed up compared to others so I won't get into specifics here. Talk to trainers and coaches to get some ideas on the best warm up procedure for you personally and get comfortable with it because it will be your battle trigger, the moves you pull and the build-up you use before it's go time.

Once you have a warm up that you are happy with you can use it all your life so don't be pressured into changing things up just for the sake of it. I pull the same emotional trigger and warm up that I have had for a long time now because it is so loaded with emotions that I can reach my peak mindset in seconds, it works.

Achieve your optimal state

When you are warming up it is important for you to understand what state of mind you want to achieve.

You already know this from the times in your past when you were at your best. That mental state you were in when you took that win or when you were on fire back then, that's the person you want to create in the present time.

So like before, if you think of the best performances that you have ever had and remember what your mindset was like, what you were focused on, what you were thinking at the time and how you would have been physically, then you have the recipe for recreating your optimal state.

Do that now, think of one of your best performances, on or off track. Something that is relevant.

Once you have it, answer these questions:

1. What were you thinking back then when you were performing at your best?

2. What mood were you in?
3. What did it feel like?
4. How were you holding your body?
5. Can you create that mental state again now?

If you do this with your eyes closed and visualize, in first person, the great times you had due to you performing well then you can teleport back there and feel it all over again.

This can actually be part of your warm up. If you show your brain the good performances then it will naturally want that again and you can instantly help it manifest the mindset it had.

This is the same when you close your eyes and revisit other good times in your life, you can feel the emotions you had and what you were experiencing back then, it puts a smile on your face. That is exactly what we are doing here.

You have had times when you were mentally at your best, remind your mind of these times and put it back into that state.

This is one of your main goals on a race weekend. You may have external goals but this internal goal is what makes the external ones achievable.

Internal always comes first so know exactly what your optimal state is and come up with ways of getting there.

Like what we did with your emotions, focus on what you need to and do with your body what you need to, to create the mind you want. Then go.

Practice this as you did with creating other emotions. Do it when you are about to play other sports, when on the sim again, when you are going into meetings and anything else where you need to be on form mentally. This will be your go to every time you want to perform at something.

One corner at a time

When in the car, to keep things simple and occupy the mind with intention, I suggest that you only focus on one corner or a single short section at a time. Concentrate the mind on what is in front of you.

It is easy for you to spend too much time worrying about lap time and other people when really you should be focused on what you are doing when in the car. Your focus needs to be on the corner that is coming up at some speed.

As you drive you are solving complex problems whilst on the go so your mind needs to be completely solution based and following simple commands. You need to allow the subconscious to help you and intuitively drive the car. The conscious is just there to help direct where the attention goes if needed.

So direct that attention on the next corner. If you make a mistake then the reaction shouldn't be to mentally beat yourself up and fall into pity mode, instead what you focus on shouldn't change and you stay disciplined to the plan and again look at the next corner.

As a performer you stay on task. You become like a robot and no matter what happens you keep focused on the objective. You must complete that lap and drive how you need to.

When a person is like this they are mentally unbeatable. They just keep going no matter what and that all comes down to what they are prioritising in their mind and what they are attempting to do.

Be that robot, keep your attention on what you want your mind to do next, corner after corner.

Everything else can be ignored whilst in qualifying.

When the time is not coming

When you are giving it your all and the lap times are still not what you want then you have a choice to make. Are you going to let it stress you out or are you going to remain resourceful?

Every driver says that they want to remain resourceful when in this situation but most are not, they lose their minds.

Your feelings of frustration, anger or even embarrassment have nothing to do with your lap time.

If you are putting too much emphasis on how you feel about your lap times or have your ego attached to them then you will always be a slave to the stopwatch.

The lap time you get is nothing more than the truth. It is yet another mathematical equation that basically shows you an outcome. The equation is:

$$\text{Driving} + \text{Car} + \text{Luck} = \text{Lap Time}$$

You need to have all these three working for you in order to create a competitive lap time. If one of them isn't performing well or not in place then the lap time will be slower. But if you have the driving down, the car is exactly how you need it and you have a sprinkling of good luck on your lap then you will reach your best outcome.

It really is that straight forward. These are just the facts of life.

So next time when you are in the car, driving your heart out and look down on your lap time and it isn't showing you any love, then you have a choice to make.

Am I going to get frustrated, overdrive and make mistakes or am I going to remember the lap time equation and get curious about how I can unlock a better outcome?

The decision really is yours whilst in the car.

Emotions can serve you in the car if they allow you to come up with solutions and be at your best, if not then they have no place in the cockpit.

I repeat, the lap time is just an outcome, it's the truth, so if you want it to improve it then focus on what you can do within your driving to either take certain corners better and drive around the handling or engine problem that the car may have.

The luck part of the equation is something you may not be able to influence much, but do what you can to make your own luck (no traffic).

I also repeat that you are the leader of all things related to your racing. As the leader you do not let a lap time dictate how you feel and allow it to be the reason for you mentally crumbling at the very time when you need to step up.

You must be solution focused and figure out the equation you need in the short time you have. These are the skills that champions possess.

Your ability to problem solve in such environments is what we stated at the beginning of this book.

Remember this next time it happens, focus your mind on what it is going to do about the situation, not how it feels about the situation.

Give it some direction, make it curiously look for solutions. Ensure that you come into the pitlane knowing that you really did try all that you could and that you are fascinated to know what else you could have done because you are just about to learn something.

When stressed in the car, snap yourself out of it using the ABC technique (described in the next chapter) and change your focus along with your physiology. It will take a few times to get this right but it needs to be done if you are to be the best you can be.

Qualifying is your time to let rip and express yourself so take what you can from this chapter and let yourself do just that.

The Mindset For Races

CHAPTER TWENTY-SIX

The Mindset For Races

"Focus and simplicity...once you get there you can move mountains"
Steve Jobs

All that we have covered in this book has been to help you build the mind you want and help you use your emotions to help you rather than harm, so you already have many tools in place that will assist you in mentally performing during a race.

But to make sure that you have everything you need and of course, to get more specific, I want to share some more training for how you can compete with the mindset you want when racing. In races we can face many challenges like:

- Being switched on and assertive on the first lap
- Regaining focus after a mistake or once being overtaken
- Maintaining confidence when in the lead or a high position
- Dealing with the pressure of a driver close behind

- Maintaining the concentration needed

We will address these and more race related topics in this chapter.

The story of a race

A race is like a story, it has a beginning, a middle and an end and the plot has many twists and turns. The character in this story, you, has to deal with the attack from others who want the same thing.

You have to answer the conundrums that are presented to you.

You have to pick yourself up, dust yourself off and go again when you take a hit in some way.

You have to outthink and outmanoeuvre the people who take you on.

You have to maintain consistency whilst all this is going on and manage the changing characteristics of your racing machine and its grip levels.

You are determined to control the plot of your story and have the ending that you want but so many things can happen that can change your intended script.

This is quite a lot for a person to do single handedly. You won't see it in this way because you once again have chunked down all of these tasks and as far as you are concerned you are just racing round a track. But in reality you are doing all of this so it is easy to understand why your mind can sometimes go into panic mode or you lose your flow when things are not going to plan.

We will start off by taking a look at the story of a typical race then I will split it up into three parts, like the plot of a film or in some ways like the stages of a fight depending on your strategy.

Obviously if you race in endurance races or in a shared car then this may differ so you will have to adjust this to suit your race format but here is the basic structure and what is required by the driver at these times.

The Beginning - On The Offence

The beginning phase of a sprint to medium length race is insightful. This is where you see the confidence and assertiveness of drivers. You get to learn who has the hunger, who is mentally switched on, who is in control of themselves and their car.

When you are good at overtaking, at seizing opportunities, have good car control and being on the offence in the opening laps then you will be directed by certain inner rules and beliefs that will help you outperform those around you.

If you have rules and beliefs like this:

- The start is when everyone is close and I can make the most of overtaking before the race settles down.
- Most drivers are mentally asleep at the start so I must pounce.
- A driver can stand out at the start of races. So it's my time shine.
- If I get drivers early, then I will dominate them mentally.

- Once I get a reputation for being a good starter and an animal of the first lap, drivers will be intimidated when they see me in the mirror and will be distracted.

When a driver has these kinds of rules and beliefs then they are dangerous (in a good way), they use it to shape their preparation, their training and their approach to a race. If you start directly in front of a driver like this and you are not ready or not mentally switched on enough, then they will always get round you.

You don't have to be over aggressive at the beginning, you just have to be an absolute ninja and execute. You need to fill the gaps that open before they close, you have to stick your car in a place that forces other drivers to give you the position and you have to get the hell out of there whilst most of the other drivers are still coming to terms with the fact that the race has started and are finding their feet still.

As you can maybe tell, I really do love this part of the race and love training drivers for it.

I get inspired by watching videos back from when Lewis Hamilton and Max Verstappen first came into F1. They had to calm down a little because they caused one or two accidents, which is easily done when in F1 because if you slightly disrupt someone in the braking area then it quickly turns into an accident. The braking distances are so short that things can get messy very quickly but this style served them massively before they reached F1.

I also like watching some of Fernando Alonso's first lap onboards. He is a driver who knows how to overtake and make the most of these opportunities. There is a fine art to applying the right blend of aggression and control. You have to be mentally present to do it and have no hesitation.

You must be focused on what is ahead, look where the drivers in front are already looking. Plan your future moves just like a Grandmaster does when playing chess.

You put your mind down the road more to help orchestrate what you want to happen in your exchange with the cars that you are pouncing on.

With the use of visualisation beforehand and with an effective warm up before you get into the car you can create the mindset and knowhow needed to be this kind of driver.

If one of your goals for a race weekend was for you to be at your best in qualifying, another one of your performance goals should be to execute on the first lap.

All of these types of goals help you take on the beliefs and have a different approach to most of the other drivers on the grid. As they are still worrying about brake shapes you are giving your mind a clear objective to execute on and this determines where your mind is at. This puts you in control rather than have situations control you.

All of these things I am repeating again because all of these things need to go into your mind and stick.

Do not go crazy at the start, you don't want to be wild you just need to stamp your authority in this phase of the race and let everyone know your intentions.

The Middle - Pure Focus

After the beginning of the race has passed and things start to settle down, other drivers will start to find their feet and then it becomes a game of cat and mouse.

Watching this next part of the race is like watching a football match when you can see the players gain, lose and regain confidence and rhythm. You can see each driver doing the same as they attempt to keep their concentration and mental clarity.

This again creates an opportunity for you because if you are good at maintaining your focus for long periods of time and if you can constantly reset your mind no matter what happens in the race then you will benefit from others who underperform in this area.

Drivers will often want to improve their concentration for this part of the race.

You will never eradicate distractions and to be honest, if your mind wanders a little from time to time then it isn't always a bad thing. You can sometimes achieve personal best lap times when you are daydreaming and driving on automatic. So I wouldn't over stress the importance of you having 100% conscious focus and by having your eyes out on stalks for the entire race.

We need to be more interested in how you can drive at one with the car and be in the flow. To remove some of the conscious thought and just let go.

Stripping things back

You often find that drivers mentally perform and drive at their best when they have stripped away all the conscious rules and concerns and simply allow themselves to just drive.

You will see this when a driver has been turned around on the first lap and they fall to dead last. All of a sudden they have no pressure on their shoulders because one of the worst outcomes has already happened, so they just think "Screw it" and they unleash themselves into the race.

You will see that driver being fuelled by the energy or determination (some call it anger) and ruthless mindset of having nothing to lose, they then throw caution to the wind and go for it. This is where the magic often happens.

They stop overthinking and if they have a good car underneath them then they put on a great show on their comeback drive.

This alone goes to show the difference that I want you to major in here. Why does a driver allow themselves to perform like that when they drop to last, compared to what they were like mentally when they were up at the sharp end?

Well it's down to the way they see the race now. They have given themselves permission to go for it and focus forward.

They no longer think about protecting a position, instead they want to get as many as they can.

This is when a driver is mentally on fire and this is an insight to the human mind.

Once you put the brain in 'Go mode' and you remove the mental baggage that causes you to consciously think about things too much, your internal processor slows down.

No longer are you that computer that is frantically spinning away on the inside and starting to overheat. Hence why I am so adamant that you simplify things down, focus on what you want and have a core performance goal.

These things allow you to quieten the mind and direct more of your subconscious mind towards what is important to you.

You will have experienced this mental freedom when playing other sports.

I notice it in Tennis when you are hitting the ball back and forth just practicing with nobody keeping score, you do some amazing shots. But then when somebody says "OK lets start now, first to six games wins", your looseness disappears, you start to miss hit the easiest of shots and before long you are verbally expressing your disgust with yourself.

From now on when this happens, I want you to be your own coach and fully understand that you are creating all of this. I want you to pause or at least debrief the whole episode after the match and find out what your thought process was when you were hitting shots that were worthy of Wimbledon, compared to what you were thinking and what your body was like when you couldn't even get the ball over the net.

It goes without saying but always do this with your racing because you really do need to learn about yourself. Know your triggers, know what it takes for you to be at your best and worst and see the patterns that you have. Once you can see a pattern and something that happens each time then you can easily change things.

This presence of mind and desire to understand your processes will be your making and will put you on another level.

Concentration or focus?

Like I briefly mentioned, when people say that they want to improve their concentration they really mean that they want to be calm, focused and confident throughout the race.

You achieve this by having the following mental skills in place:

Dealing with mental hang-ups you have about yourself - If you lack self-belief, if you worry too much about what others think, if you have things from your past that are still holding you back or have other concerns, then these can creep up on you when you least want them.

We all have some of these things but if they are affecting you when competing then deal with them away from the circuit before you compete. These are the measures you need to go to if you want to mentally tune yourself and make sure that you are at your best.

Being armed with mental techniques you can use on the go - You will be subject to things in a race that were not part of the plan or do not happen as you want, when this happens then you need the ability to bring your mind back in line and keep it focused on the original personal performance objectives.

Having objectives and goals that are process based - Set up the game to win. If you go into a race with only one goal and that is to win, then once that doesn't become possible for some reason then your mind will not have direction and it will either capitulate or kick into panic mode. It will be unsure what to do and based upon your internal coding it could react in a number of ways.

To focus forward when other cars are distracting you - This largely refers to when you are being caught and pressured from a driver behind, when another car is getting larger and filling your mirrors. When a driver can see that you are looking in your mirror and they see that you are now starting to drive defensively, you are feeding them the confidence they need to keep attacking.

They steal your mental strength, before you know it they dominate your mind and overtake you. This is something that can be avoided if you master the next point.

Know what percentage of your mind is driving - This brings us back to - 'Where the focus goes the energy flows'. What you focus on is what you get.

So when you look in the mirrors or think about what others will say then that is what you attract and what you allow to flood your mind. As a driver you know that where you look is where you go, and that goes for your mind also. So be aware of what you are focusing on and how much of it (percentage wise) is actually on driving each corner that is coming up and how much of your attention is being wasted elsewhere.

Accessing your peak mental state - When you are in the flow, in your peak mental state, it's as if most of your awareness widens but it is still directed to help you move forward and you use your intuition more. You feel in control. When you are fully in the zone then 'It' drives, 'It' takes over. 'It' being the true you and when your mind is at one with the task in hand. This state of mind is the ultimate goal for a driver, it's when you get out of the way.

These are all areas that you need to work on and spend your time mastering. This may seem a lot but once you fully take on what has been taught so far in this book and you dedicate yourself to train this part of your racing game then this is easily achievable.

It may look daunting and you can understand why so many drivers cannot even be bothered to work on these things but mentally improving yourself day by day is your key to being able to race with the emotional control and mindset that you need.

The End - The Knockout

The end of the race is another interesting time to witness a mental shift in drivers.

You may see the leader start to make mistakes because they are in the classic mental trap of not wanting to screw up, so in having that goal, they all of a sudden tense up and under-drive.

Or you start to see lunges from the drivers who have been waiting patiently until the last few laps. Which as a knock on effect causes the drivers who are in front of them to over-defend and then it all kicks off.

Some drivers need to pounce, others need to think strategically, this cocktail is another opportunity for the mental game to play a factor.

To get the best out of yourself in this situation you need to maintain the forward focus and self-belief that you hopefully had mid race. To direct the mind to think of the next corner coming up and to recall what was the most important aspect of each corner. If you start to brake too late for the corners that you need good exits for, then you will be easy prey for the other drivers.

So remind yourself of what is important and focus like you do on a qualifying lap if you need to.

Mental techniques for races

Now that you can see the different skills that you need and have hopefully been inspired with a few ideas of your own, I want to run you through some mental techniques that you can use to help you in all stages of a race.

I am going to blast a load of small and big techniques at you now, you can do all or choose the ones that you like. Use this like a menu.

Heck, even create your own techniques.

Start with a clear performance related goal

I thought I would mention this again due to its importance because it is easy to get carried away with being results driven.

When going into a race, give your mind a goal, or goals, that it can directly execute on. If you want to win then what performance goals can you give yourself in order to achieve that win.

What process goals can you set?

Here are a few that might inspire your thoughts:

- Keep my vision forward and up
- Dominate everyone on the first lap
- Encourage myself with a smile each new lap I start
- Breathe and relax
- Always get good exits on turns 2, 5 and 10
- Look in early and hit apexes
- When stressed, I refocus within 10 seconds

These are just examples but if you know the kinds of things that you falter on once you lose focus, and they then slow you down, tell the brain what to do and it will do it.

Your performance or process goal needs to be clear, achievable and give you small wins throughout the race. The brain likes progress so having these types of goals will make it feel encouraged and keep you calmer.

Reach your peak state with your Pre-Race Routine

Back to priming again, you need a warm up routine that puts you into the state of mind that you need. This is a given but must be done so you can show up how you want to at the start at least.

Focus on what you want to achieve and become the person you were when you achieved some of your greatest performances in the past. Think how you thought back then, hear what you heard and mimic the physiology that goes along with that state of mind.

Maintain that physiology as you walk to your car in the pit, awning or collection area. You want to be wearing your emotions on the outside. Recall what Mike Tyson said in the fear chapter, watch the video of his ring walk on YouTube, understand what that does to your opposition when they see you walking to the car like that.

They will clearly see that you mean business and so will your mind.

Remember that your mind is always waiting for instructions for what emotions you want. If you want to be confident then walk to your car in a confident way. Become that super hero.

Then get into your car that you have visualised as a bright light and as your armour. Believe that each time the belt strap is tightened you get stronger and stronger, more confident and determined.

By the time you select first gear you are the warrior you need to be. Then you get out onto that track armed with your simple process goals and you execute.

As you can see, all of this is starting to come together now, you are becoming the warrior.

Feel good on the warm up laps

As you are out warming tyres and going to the grid, purposely feel good about what you are doing. Put a proud and strong look on your face, nod your head and feel the rhythm of the track.

Use this warm up as an extended part of your warm up routine and activate the mind to get excited for what you are about to do.

Remind yourself of how lucky you are and how proud you are of this moment and embrace it. This can be as fantastic as you want it to be. You are racing for goodness sake, how amazing is that really?

Get into a good mood and enjoy this.

On the driving side, drive the ideal race lines on a few of the important corners because next time you come through you will be racing so it's good to give your mind one last heads up.

Check out any puddles if it is wet and use the lap for everything you can for both mental and driving purposes.

First lap vision

As you start, no matter how good or bad the start is, always look forward, keep your eyes up and plan your way through those in front if you are not in front already.

Get your head ahead of where you are and look for opportunity. With the goals you have and the eyes looking forward your mind has no other option but to provide you with information that will help you forward. So use this simple vision technique to guide you to where you want to go.

Use breathing each lap

It is easy for you to become tense when in a race, to put too much effort in and hardly breathe. This is the physiology of someone who is under attack and not relaxed.

You know that to drive at your best you need to be firm with your inputs but you also need to be relaxed. So instead of mimicking a tense person, take a nice deep breath in and breathe smoothly out as you go down the straight or start a new lap.

This can act as a nice little reset or a way to keep yourself in check. Plus you need oxygen so if you are stressing then you may even forget to breathe as much as you need to. This happens a lot.

The ABC Technique

Here is one of my favourites. This technique is like your emergency button for when you are emotionally out of control or have created a mindset that isn't helping you and you want to get back to a good state of mind again.

This is all about interrupting your pattern. If breathing alone isn't cutting it then the ABC technique will if done correctly.

A stands for Acknowledge It
B stands for Break It
C stands for Change It

To show you how this works, let's say that you have just gotten into a good position but due to you feeling uncomfortable because it is higher than you have ever been before and you don't want to screw it up, you tighten up and lose your rhythm.

You may start looking in the mirror and worry about all kinds of things related to external things (like what people will say if you do screw up).

It is plain to see that the very mindset that got you into that position and helped you drive in an impressive way, has gone from offence mode to defence mode. Now you are in a protective state of mind and no longer driving as well as you did, and you need to snap out of it to regain control.

First Acknowledge It

First of all you acknowledge and realise that you are in a mindset that you don't want.

Don't just carry on being frantic, actually say out loud, "Oh, I see what's happening here", or anything else that acknowledges this emotion.

If you can give this mindset a funny name beforehand, like Wimpy William, you can literally say "Oh hello Wimpy William".

In doing something like this you have alerted the mind that it is in the incorrect mode and it needs to be put back to how it was. It is mocking it in a way, which also helps you feel in control again.

Then Break it

Immediately after that I want you to do something that breaks you out of that current crappy mindset.

If you were in normal life and you were sitting down feeling sad, then I would get you to rapidly stand up so you nearly get a head rush, then throw your arms in the air and shout "I LOVE THIS LIFE" with a huge smile on your face.

This is what you call radically breaking the pattern.

A rapid shift in your physiology and what you are thinking completely disrupts what you were thinking about and how you were holding yourself before.

It's a dramatic way of what we do all the time when we are about to say something but then someone interrupts us, then we can't remember what we were going to say.

Obviously you cannot stand up in your chair as you are racing so you have to come up with your own way of doing this.

I have had drivers doing all kinds of things for this, some have smacked their visor with the palm of their hand to shock themselves out of it, some have burst out laughing and I've even had some say outlandish things like "There are poor kids are starving in Africa".

Yes these are a bit out there but they are all used to snap them out of the self defeating emotions or mood that they are in. The last one about kids starving is not to mock or be derogatory in any way, a driver just came up with that because in his mind it would not only be a strange thought to break his pattern and interrupt his thought process, but it would also remind him how lucky he is to be racing. This worked for him.

Your aim here is to shock the brain and temporarily confuse it. Once done you quickly move onto the last phase.

Then Change It

Once your mind is in a state of "What now?" due to you breaking it's pattern, you quickly align your focus and your physiology with the emotions you want.

So if you want to get back to your confident state of mind you might:

1. Put your confident face on.
2. Shout out loud in your drill sergeant voice "Next!", which tells your brain to focus forward on the next corner.

3. You sit and hold the wheel in a confident way, as much as you can with the belts on.
4. You put your chin up.
5. And you direct your mind with clear instructions of what to do next and coach yourself into the mindset that you want.

That's it

It may sound like a lot but you can do all of this in a matter of five seconds, and the more you do this the better you get.

That is why I want you to always practice going from one emotion to another at will because it is a skill that serves massively when racing. This is something you can play with and get something that works for you and works every time.

Again you can condition this on the simulator, when playing other sports or when you are just about to go into a business meeting.

You are the one who controls your emotions or at least have that belief and this will serve you. Condition it, use it and benefit from it.

The word 'Next'

I have found that the word 'Next' works well. If you just shout or say this word with intent when you are driving then it can help you regain your focus.

It is your way of telling the brain what to focus on, like the next corner or the next car that you want to catch and in doing so you have just put a carrot out in front of the donkey.

This is kind of like a condensed version, albeit less effective version, of the ABC technique because in stating "Next" you are snapping your mind out of its current thought process and telling it what to look at.

Simple but effective.

Mickey Mouse

Lastly I want to re-introduce you to Mickey Mouse. This is another mental strategy that is a bit crazy but can work well.

Have you ever had times when you hear the words of a parent or someone else who has said things like "You are not good enough" or "You will get beaten", etc?

The echo of someone else's negativity can come into your mind at the worst times. It may even sound like your voice in your head but at some point, someone else put that there.

If you have and these thoughts come into your mind when you are already sinking mentally, then they can compound the mental pit that you have fallen into. But Mickey Mouse can help save the day.

This is only a quick fix but can work like magic for some people.

You will have done this as a kid when your parents said something like "I hope you have cleaned your room" and as the kid you were, you would repeat what they said in a funny voice and mock them.

That is exactly what the Mickey Mouse technique is all about. If you have self-talk or thoughts that are not helping you at critical times, then you can mock them by repeating them in the stupidly high pitched Mickey Mouse voice.

I told you that this was a crazy strategy.

This is just your way of not taking the defeating self-belief or thought seriously and you are sapping the power out of it. It doesn't need to be Mickey Mouse; it can be another voice that you find funny. The funnier the better.

When you do this you are changing the feelings that you associate to those thoughts and it is astonishing how such a simple technique can work.

Summary

Please go through this chapter again to see what works for you and see what clever ways you can come up with to create your own mental strategies and techniques.

Changing emotions and behaviours is largely all about breaking your automatic patterns and refocusing the mind on something else or a different action, so as long as you stick to that fundamental then you can do all sorts.

Come up with a game plan for each phase of your races and have this performance process running alongside your actual driving. This is just like what a warrior does with a battle and what a boxer does when planning their strategy for a fight. They split it up and have game plans, then train with that game plan in mind.

Drivers don't normally think about approaching races in this way.

If you crack this and find something that works for you then it won't be long until people are asking you how you stay so calm, motivated or confident. They won't understand how you remain resilient when faced with challenges and it will all be because you are mastering your emotions and creating the mindset you want. Plus you know how to read and approach a race.

That is one of the success secrets that will help you in all parts of your life.

That's your Warrior's Mind.

Handling Teammates, Jealousy & Criticism

CHAPTER TWENTY-SEVEN

Handling Teammates, Jealousy & Criticism

"
"To avoid criticism, do nothing, say nothing
and be nothing"
Elbert Hubbard

I wanted to do this chapter because even though our main objective is to help you as an individual, you know all too well that other people play a big role in your racing.

Without other people, who will prepare your car, who will sponsor you, who will help you improve, who will support you, who will compete against you and who will even grant you a race licence in the first place.

People are great, we like them, love them and we need them.

However there are certain times when people can be a proper pain in the backside and can knock you off your game. That is what I want to speak about here.

When it comes to people we could have gone deep here and talked about your girl or boyfriends and how to handle your personal life but that will be for another book or I will cover that on The Race Driver Coach Show.

Here I want to talk about the kind of things that every race driver will face in most seasons and give you some very quick tips on each.

Ego

This short word can mean different things but for the purpose of this subject I am referring to ego as a person's self-esteem or self-importance.

Race drivers often wrap their ego up with their results, they attach who they are as a person by the results they get.

If they beat you on track they then see themselves as literally being a better individual than you. If they earn more money than you then they believe that they are more worthy.

Most drivers really do care what other people think and it affects them. They are so used to being told that "You are only as good as your last result" or "If you win then you get to advance in some way", so no wonder they feel this way, they link their identity to the results they get.

I know that can be said for many sports but if you add this on to the environment that we have in racing where you can pay for better equipment or for a more competitive team, then you have a sport that has hardly any competitors who possess the Warrior's Mind.

Their ego's create a serious mental weakness when threatened, and one thing that this sport is good at is creating situations that expose drivers.

I am not saying that all drivers are like this, but it is common to see.

Teammates

When a new teammate joins a team the other drivers obviously feel as though their ego may be under threat. They can think the worst and worry that their teammates could be quicker than them or will get on better with the team.

This causes an interesting environment to compete in because we share the same team as another driver and we are forced to call them teammates but to be honest, unless you are racing in endurance championships and sharing your car with someone, then they are not really teammates because you are competing against each other for the championship.

You may be a little bit more careful around them in the race because you do not want to hit them and be told off by the team boss or have an atmosphere back at the truck, but that's about it.

I have had drivers that want to mentally screw up their teammates in order to get the edge over them so they play all sorts of mental games, but that doesn't really work.

I have had drivers that are a bit too friendly with their teammates, but that also doesn't work.

So to maybe help you in this area I want to give you some pointers for what I have seen work best.

The best words of advice I could possibly give you on this subject is to have no ego.

If you follow what we have done in this book then you will have a Matrix that is solely focused on reaching your North Star, that has a Towards Value called of progress, that has beliefs that only make you stronger with every defeat, that is hungry for knowledge and understands that each challenge is needed to improve your skills.

If you stick to that way of seeing things and genuinely create your Warrior's Mind then having a new teammate in your team will be welcomed by you.

You need them to be quick in order to make you learn faster and keep pushing you forward.

You need to improve your mental skills so you need a teammate that will test you in that way.

Ayrton Senna would not have been as impressive if he didn't have Alain Prost there in the same team. They drove each other to higher levels.

That's no different with you.

A quick teammate who may even have a challenging personality, will only improve you. Due to you thinking of the long game, that will serve you a lot more than having some backmarker as a teammate.

Together you will improve the car, you will take points from your other rivals and you will be forced to prepare more and get more from yourself.

If your parents are fuelling the fire by complaining about your teammates and the treatment they are getting compared to you or are being nasty about them, do not allow yourself to fall for that. You see it for the opportunity that it is and know that if you make it through the year using your teammates as indirect coaches of yours, then you will prosper.

If they beat you then you learn.

If you beat them then so what? You keep focusing forward.

So avoid having a point scoring, "I am better than you" relationship with your teammates. It is taxing on the mind, wastes energy and is just your ego running the show if you do this. It makes you mentally weak and easily beatable.

The side benefit

When you are not being affected by your teammates, that alone usually knocks them off their game because you don't react to their intentional mind games. The more they beat you the more you keep coming for them. The more you beat them the more you keep working to forge forward.

When you are competing against someone who is not affected by your efforts and results it is like taking on a terminator. It is difficult to get the reaction you want and will distract you if you are an 'ego' driver.

Instead keep seeing it as a Warrior would and use every challenge to build you more. If you keep this outlook then you will be exactly what manufacturers and top teams will want.

That's the other side benefit of not possessing a delicate ego.

If you keep working with the long game in mind and take your losses with dignity, if you live by your warrior code then you will impress the pants off people in this sport. These are all leadership traits that every team wants and what you need if you are going to reach your North Star.

Jealousy

Jealousy is experienced by drivers in two main ways.

You have people being jealous of you and reacting to that.

Then there is you being jealous of others and letting that bother you.

The former is something that you cannot really do anything about. If you are getting the results, the opportunities and the offers to advance that make others jealous then that is their problem. It's out of your control and is just a sign that you are doing well.

Expect people to be jealous of you at times. Do not let it feed your ego, just understand that it is a normal emotion and reaction that people feel when they see others doing well and they are not happy with their own progress. That's all there is to it.

However, when it comes to you being jealous of other drivers who may be getting the shots that you want to get, once again that is the ego popping up.

Just because one driver is getting their shot, doesn't mean that you won't get yours. There is plenty to go around.

Actually, when another driver gets a win or gets promoted through the sport then you should bloody celebrate because it shows that the system of progression in motorsport works. If it worked for them then it will work for you if you seize the opportunities that come your way, if you have the speed and if you promote yourself well.

At ties sports, like life, are not fair. I know so many great drivers who do not get the chance they deserve. If you are being ignored by the industry then it's because you are not being seen or you are not creating a reason for them to select you.

When someone you have beat gets a dream offer then take a look at your results, behaviour, quality of your management, your image and anything else that would have caused you to be overlooked.

Remember, you are the CEO, so if your 'company' isn't producing the product you need then it's up to you to find out why and make some changes.

So all in all, jealousy is another waste of time and not the trait of a warrior. So if you feel it then ask why, what Avoidance Value is this triggering and deal with it practically.

Jealousy is an emotion like any other, when you feel it, understand what your mind is telling you and then translate it to help you work better or harder.

Other people's success has nothing to do with you, they are on their own journey. So keep your nose out of it and focus on you.

Criticism

Criticism is very closely related to jealousy. It is another thing that you will experience as you climb the ladder.

I mean come on, how many people criticise great sportsmen and women like Michael Schumacher, Michael Jordan, Serena Williams and Muhammad Ali. Total genius' in their sports yet they will have more critics than most others.

People are completely entitled to have their opinion and if you go back to how a person's Matrix works then you will understand that a person's viewpoints, beliefs and the way they translate things, forms their opinions.

So how can you take the opinions of others to heart?

People just take a snapshot of a certain situation, then they make a throwaway comment based on the mental filters they are looking through. It's just how things look from their angle.

When you take this on and see what criticism is then you cannot take it seriously. We all make comments about people from time to time with very little thought or weight to those comments.

A great Les Brown quote I want you to remember on this topic is:

Other people's opinions of you does not have to become your reality

This is not just a pump up motivational quote, this is fact. Les Brown had to endure serious criticism and ridicule himself and it held him back for many years. Until one day he decided to live by this and many other supporting beliefs and it released him.

As I just said then, these quotes I am putting up for you are not empty quotes, they are the beliefs of people who have gotten more out of themselves and this is us modelling them.

Travel light

I want you to travel light. Do not carry around the heavy thoughts of others, do not let jealousy or criticisms weigh you down because it will only prevent you from progressing up that mountain.

You have to slay many dragons on the way to your North Star so you cannot even think about what other people say because you are too busy and need to get going.

Also ignore the good comments

If you want to genuinely reduce the impact that other people's opinions and actions have on you, you also need to let all the good comments affect you less.

We all like to be told that we are doing well and get praise but be careful because that feeds the ego. If you are addicted to getting praise then you will be more affected when you get criticised.

This is linked to people who over celebrate a win, they are usually the people who take losses very badly.

As a Warrior it is your job to stay centred most of the time. Staying centred means that you do not crave admiration from others too much, you do not boast when you win.

Then as a result you will automatically take losses better and will deal with criticism better.

I know this all may be a strange way of seeing things, because as we grew up our parents would punish us when we did something wrong and they celebrated when we did something right.

At school if we were admired and praised by our friends then we were considered as cool, and if we were criticised then it was deeply embarrassing. This has stuck with us and created a mental craving for the admiration and approval of others.

As a warrior you just do the prep, train your mind so it is purpose built, turn up and go further than anyone else is prepared to go. Then you perform as you can and go home.

You then do this over and over again until you reach your pot of gold or find another path along the way.

It may sound unemotional when I say it that way but don't worry, emotions will always be a part of this to a certain extent, you are human.

Get Back On That Horse

CHAPTER TWENTY-EIGHT

Get Back On That Horse

> **"**
>
> *"Every setback has a major comeback"*
> *Russell Wilson*

I wanted to put this chapter in at the end because it has to be said that you can do all the mental training you want, you can be getting the results you want, but there will always be a time when life happens to you and you lose your mojo or have something that knocks you off your game.

This is the yoyo of life.

Just when things are going well and you think you have things down; the universe can throw you a curveball that causes you to question yourself and as a result it drains your motivation.

Well in this chapter I want to speak from my heart and give you something to read when you are losing hope and need to get back on that horse.

Climbing the mountain to your North Star

We call it a climb when you are travelling to your North Star for a reason. When climbing up a mountain you have to persevere no matter what weather passes through.

As you get higher there are less people because it is hard to get to that point then you start to face opposition who are just as tough and as skilled as you.

You will have boulders fall on you that know you back, you will sometimes be on loose ground that is risky to walk on so you must slow down, and you can get to unpassable parts of your chosen route so you have to turn back and try another way.

The tough climb isn't for everyone, it is only a special few that can make it all the way.

Winter will hit

Due to you being on your climb to your North Star for such a long period of time you will experience some harsh winters.

Wall Street refers to economic downturns as winters. They know it's going to come, they know that it will be rough but if they can stay the course, be patient and prepare for when things get back to normal then they will not only survive the winter but they will be able to scoop up all the leftovers from those who perished during it.

Something that we have always seen in our lifetimes is that spring and summer always follow winter. As reliable as the sun is at coming up each morning we know that sooner or later things will get better in life and we will resume.

Just like the COVID-19 pandemic that began back in 2019, when the whole world was on standstill, when people lost their livelihoods and their lives, we all knew that one day we would find our way through it and would eventually come out the other side.

It sometimes takes a lot longer than we think but the collective faith just goes to show that as humans we always know that things can get better. We always find a way through and summer will always come again.

I want you to remember this no matter what you are going through because as devastating things can be at times, things are temporary.

You are stronger than any challenge that can be thrown at you.

Billy Monger and Alex Zanardi

You only have to look at people like Billy Monger and Alex Zanardi. Here are two race drivers who had their legs amputated due to two horrific accidents in their race cars.

They could have easily lost their lives but luckily for all of us their hearts kept pumping and so did their love for the sport that hurt them so much.

Both drivers ended up coming back to racing and won races. Alex Zanardi actually went on to win the Italian Superturismo Championship, he won World Touring Car Championship races and even got a gold medal in the Paralympics. Unfortunately, he had another accident whilst on his bike in Italy but these drivers demonstrated how you can endure your toughest winter and come out the other side if you are willing to fight.

These are not special human beings, these are people like you and me but they are people who decided to not bow down to circumstances when they were thrust into their dark times.

They have shown that there are drivers out there with the lion hearts and warrior minds.

You

I know that no matter what you have gone through you can always find your way though.

If COVID-19 caused your sponsors to pull out on you at short notice, if you had an accident that stopped you racing or if you are losing hope because you are not getting where you want then I want you to understand, really understand, that it is never too late to turn things around.

If you feel like you are bashing your head up against a brick wall and getting nowhere, that is just life's way of saying "Change your approach and try again".

You have this goal in motorsport to give you purpose, to help you achieve the life you want and to help you build into a more capable human being. This is a journey for you, it is a seriously tough climb but it is giving you something that makes you feel alive. It can be a one sided love story at times but the way it forces you to be relentless is what a warrior lives for.

It's a worthwhile challenge and you have your short life time to give it all you have.

If you have a goal to become or remain a professional driver then you have to be willing to take the hits, and a lot of them. You have to take a truthful look at yourself (like we did earlier but even more thorough) and see what things you are simply not good enough at the moment and find out ways to improve or change your direction.

If you truly give this everything you have then you will either make it to your original goal or will end up wherever you were supposed to be. Either way you will know and you will rest easy because you genuinely gave it your all.

What I want to get across is that this will be tough but it will be worth it. I want you to know that it will seem impossible at times but there will be an unlock to the next level somewhere, you just have to keep searching and have the mind of a warrior to remain relentless.

There is always a way no matter how difficult things seem. If you change your perceptions, see things from different angles, use your imagination and treat this whole journey as a solvable puzzle then you will find that unlock.

One of my hits

One of the biggest hits I took in racing was when I actually achieved my North Star at the time and that was to become a British Touring Car Driver. My original North Star was to get to F1 but that had to change when I saw that I wasn't getting anywhere near that.

It was early 2001 and my teammate was going to be Carl Fogarty who was switching from bike racing.

I was already named in Autosport as one of the team's drivers and I was in the team's headquarters signing the contract.

Words really cannot describe what I was feeling. It was kind of a mixture of excitement, anxiety, disbelief and amazement all wrapped up into one emotion that resided in the centre of my chest.

I could barely breathe, and my hand was slightly shaking as I signed the contract.

Then before the ink could dry, a new member of the management who also wanted to race my car walked through, saw me signing it and said to the boss, Enzo's not driving the car.

Even though the boss gave me his word and even though I did all he asked me to do with my results the year previous, he went back on his word to not upset the new manager and that was it, I was out.

I haven't thought of that moment much for over a decade but as I write it I can feel some of the pain I would have had back then. That poor kid. He did everything he could, he worked his tail off and got so close.

I don't feel angry about it anymore, I just feel sorry for that young Enzo at the time, he was crushed.

When I look back now it was obviously a blessing in disguise because I wouldn't be living the life I have now, I wouldn't have met my wife and who knows, if I had got that chance at that young age I could have messed it up due to my inexperience or I could have been going to a race weekend one day and could have got run over on the road and killed.

I know that sounds twisted but I really mean that. If I was given the chance again I wouldn't change a thing, I see it as a lucky escape and thank God that I went the route I did.

The lesson

I tell you this because I want you to know that another reason I can rest easy is because I know that I gave it my absolute all. What I didn't allow for was a little bit of bad timing or bad luck that robbed me at that particular time.

But that's life, it will test you like that. When it happens it is painful but then many years later you get to see it for the gift it was. Like we said before, it serves you.

As long as you give it your all and go full throttle to your North Star then you will be happy with the outcome, I promise.

Life is a journey and some of the adjustments and turns you make are made because of some painful experiences at the time, but in the end, as I always say... it plays out.

You just make sure that you have a blast trying and see where you end up.

Loss of Motivation

If you are low on motivation at these times then there is some good news for you because motivation, like confidence, is nothing more than an emotion.

You can create it whenever you want, you can call upon it with the emotion skills that you have learned.

Your mind will become motivated when you have associated enough pain and pleasure to the situation.

If you want to feel motivated to do something then you will only move once the pain is strong enough to make you move and if the pleasure of achieving something is pleasurable enough to compel you.

Show your mind what you are here for, wake up your inner warrior on a consistent basis and make sure that they take the reins. You have to show your mind how important it is and it will step up and take on the fight.

Motivation is great but you need to be the warrior who takes action no matter how they feel. If you are feeling motivated then that is nice but the real skill is doing what needs to be done without it.

If you can take action when you don't feel like it then you will fill those time gaps that you would have not used before.

You will be working whilst your competitors are sleeping and you will be preparing for that soldier who is training in the cave to beat you.

The work that goes into attaining your North Star is not all exciting stuff to do, you will have to do weeks on end of tough work with no immediate reward. Learn how to enjoy that part of the process by knowing that nobody else will be doing it so you will have the edge come race day.

Mastering your craft is relentless but to be a warrior you must be relentless; it is a big part of your coding. You must be relentless whilst in battle and whilst in preparation.

Summary

If you have taken a hit, then get up.

If you have been dealt a bad hand, then get up.

If you are emotionally down, then get up.

You have all the resources you need within you as you read this, the only thing you need is the permission to go for it.

Guess who that permission needs to come from?

Bonus Technique: The Identity Split

CHAPTER TWENTY-NINE

Bonus Technique: The Identity Split

Oh wait, before we finish, I want to slip in one more mental training technique that can help you create the warrior mind that you want.

This is actually one of my favourite techniques to use with drivers, executives, athletes, myself and anybody else who wants to make sure that they keep on top of their mindset on a daily basis.

As you can tell I have called it the Identity Split.

To teach you this mental strategy I will explain the problem that we face, the objective of the Identity Split and then teach you how to use it.

The problem

I take the view that all of us have split personalities, one day we are on fire and crush the day being the kind of warrior we need to be, then on other days we have completely lost the motivation or mood that we need to be in.

For drivers this can happen in the car as much as out of it. You can hit the lap time and driving standard of your life on one weekend only to completely be off your game the next. This is the same for when you are working on things at home; you may have a day when you call up five sponsors, workout, update all of your social media accounts, call your team, have a zoom meeting with your manager and have a super productive day on Tuesday, but then Wednesday you can't even be bothered to email anyone, and you spend two hours straight scrolling through TikTok.

The mindset seems to have automatically changed and there is no answer for why.

The objective

The objective with the Identity Split technique is to help you take control of what mindset you are in so you can become the person you need to be on any given day or moment.

It is also a technique that can help you learn a lot about yourself and the way you operate.

As you know from previous chapters, we create emotions through our thoughts (what we are focusing on) and by the way we operate our body (our physiology). We use different combinations of each to access different emotions.

Well this is taking that principle a step further.

This time we will get clear on what you are thinking whilst you are at your best, then in contrast to that, what you are thinking when you are at your 'worst'.

Then we will give each of those mindsets an identity of it's own.

So let's say that you have spent a day feeling low on motivation and you just can't be bothered to do anything. We will quickly look at how you may have created that mindset (or what things need to be present) and then give that mindset a name.

This is you getting to know your different personalities. Once you know all about them and they have their different identity, then you can use that information to jump from one to the other.

If you have watched the film called Split, you will see Kevin (James McAvoy) going through all his personalities throughout the film, and each one has their own name.

We will do the same for you but in a controlled and productive way. Our goal here is to help you understand what is internally going on when you are in certain moods. This then gives you the information you need to mentally coach yourself.

The process

To start with, you will need a pen and a blank piece of paper for this. I have obviously put a template for you on our website should you need it.

To make this easy to understand I will describe this in steps for you to follow.

Here we go:

1. Split the page into two equal halves by drawing a line down the middle of the page, top to bottom. So now you have a left and a right-hand column.

2. You will use the left-hand column to list out the details of what you are like when you are not at your best. Then we will use the right-hand column to explain what you are like when you are completely at your best mentally.

3. Please leave a gap at the top of each column because that is where we will put the name for each personality later.

4. Think of the mindset that you do not like, the one that causes you to underperform and will never be able to reach your North Star. The certain character that is going to cause you to fail.

5. Starting with the left-hand column, I want you to list out all the traits of when you are in that mood. So if you are in a lazy mood, list out what your thoughts are, what you are focusing on, what you are saying to yourself, what is present or happening around you, how you feel, etc. The different things that are present internally and externally to allow that mindset to be created. Basically, list out the full recipe that causes that lazy mood.

6. Then I want you to think of a time when you were at your absolute best. You performed as you wanted, and you felt good. The kind of mindset you would like to have in a bottle because you would increase your chances of success if you could be that character each day.

7. Next, write out what you were thinking, focusing on, feeling and anything else that will help you understand how that mindset was achieved. This again is your recipe for creating that mindset. What thoughts and self-talk are going on in your mind when you are at your best? List it all out on the right-hand side column.

8. Now you have two mindsets, and you can see the start of a list for each of them. This needs to become your manual

for how to create each one, these are actual ingredients you can consciously put together to cook up the mindset you want.

9. Give the character on the left-hand side, a name. Give them a name that mocks them, that belittles the personality and sums them up well. So if this mindset is one that causes you to have lack of confidence and fears taking action, then you can call that personality something like 'Limp Larry' or 'Wimpy William'. Whatever name causes a smile as you say it. Write that name in the space at the top of the left column.

10. Lastly, name the character on the right-hand side column. This person needs the kind of name that a superhero would have. If this is when you are mentally on fire, then you can call that person something like 'Dan the Destroyer' or 'Mighty Megan'.

In front of you now, you have two identities. On the left is the name of the person that describes your 'under-performing mindset' and the recipe for creating them.

Then on the right you have the name of the person who you want to be more often. This is basically the name you are going to give to your warrior mind. If you can incorporate your own first or second name in this then that is good.

How it works

In doing this, you have given yourself the clarity to help you become sensitive to, and distinguish, who is in control at particular times.

By naming your different personalities and giving them separate identities, plus knowing how you contribute to creating them, gives you a lot of power.

This is linked to the ABC Technique because it helps you become aware of each mental mode (your – A for awareness).

Once you know how you mentally create the person you want and don't want, you have the power to switch.

You may have a certain set of songs that you listen to, do certain things with your body, visit specific memories, focus on things that take your mind to where it needs to be, remind yourself of something, have a particular tonality to your self-talk that say words that get you into the mood you want.

It is up to you to create the identity you want at any given moment and to do that you need to know how and what to do. This is your road map for doing that.

Every time you want to initiate Dan the Destroyer you pull your listed internal and external triggers and bring him back.

Think back to the times

To assist you in getting an accurate recipe for creating each identity, think back to moments when you were at your best and at your worst.

Mentally revisit those times individually and recall what you were thinking and focusing on when experiencing those mindsets.

If today you felt like you had no motivation or were the character that you don't want to be, then there will be a reason for that. As the sole investigator of your own mind, find out why.

You will have been viewing things in a certain way, you will have said certain things to yourself and your focus would have caused that mental state. Maybe someone else previously said something to you and you were replaying their comments, or you spent time thinking of things that were not helping you. Or you didn't have a clear goal today. There are many factors but you need to find them out.

This is your recipe. Learn from the good and the bad times and put together your road map for them.

Pull the triggers

Once you have your road map and you have named that warrior mental state, pull the triggers you need (from your recipe) and put that person back in control.

Think what you need to think about, focus on what need to focus on, have the required physiology and create that warrior.

You have to do this consciously and purposefully to start with but the better you get at it, and the more that your mind can see that it is working (and that you are in control), the more automatic this will become.

Use techniques like this and the ones that were mentioned earlier to put you back in control.

CHARGE!

Chapter Thirty

CHARGE!

You have made it.

You have reached the end of the Warrior's Mind. Wow that has been some journey.

I really don't want to stop writing because it feels like I almost know you now but I must stop otherwise this book will never be finished and will not make it into your hands.

I hope that there is at least one thing that you can take from this book, something you can run with that will help you get more from yourself as you take on the racing world.

I don't know what parts from this book stood out for you, but my top five things are:

1. Priming your days
2. Kaizen
3. Where the focus goes the energy flows
4. Be a master translator
5. Master your emotions

If you only spend your time keeping these up then you will be one tough driver to face.

My leaving thought

As a leaving thought I want you to know that I can associate with you and feel the desire that you have to reach your racing dreams. At times you will feel misunderstood by people around, you may experience times when nobody seems to understand but just know that you are never on your own.

Being a warrior on a quest can always get lonely but along the way you will meet and pick-up people to join your army. People who will share the load, who will bring skills that you miss and together you will forge forward to each other's North Stars.

Make sure that you stay true to yourself, that you work tirelessly and give this dream of yours a genuine shot.

No more half measures, no more questioning yourself, from now on it is just pure execution, day after day.

You will have to slay many dragons both internally and externally, you will have to overcome huge obstacles that attempt to block your way, but this is what you live for.

You are in a game where the difficulty level is set to high, you are attempting to compete at Expert Level, so it will not be easy. Just remember that you are a human and what you are aiming for is within your capability.

If you remain self-aware so you can see what you are good at and what you need help with, and you keep walking towards your North Star then you will either make it or you will have an absolute blast trying.

Either way, you will get a good story from it.

I want to read about you in the media, I want to see you working hard on your social media and I want to see you on that top step.

Keep believing, keep fighting for what you want and allow your Warrior Mind to help you make it happen.

I wish you all the best on your first quest.

Now get out of here, you've got work to do.

CHAAAAAARGE!

Made in the USA
Middletown, DE
14 June 2022

67128079R00208